THE
NOBEL
PRIZE

We are most grateful
for the kind support from the Nobel Foundation
with special thanks to Margaretha Ehrén
for her invaluable assistance.

PETER WILHELM

THE NOBEL PRIZE

STOCKHOLM 1983

THE NOBEL PRIZE

Editorial research:
Maj-Britt Neuman

Photo:
Peter Gullers

Cover:
David Hillman,
Pentagram Design Ltd

First published 1983
Springwood Books, London

ISBN: 0 86254 111 5

CONTENTS

ALFRED NOBEL – THE INVENTOR WHO CREATED THE NOBEL PRIZE

Alfred Nobel has often been described as the man nobody knew – in spite of the fact that his inventions, including dynamite, were linked with spectacular events during the whole latter part of the 19th century. It is no exaggeration to say that Nobel's inventions were precursory among the rapid developments that took place within industry and communication.

In modern times, Alfred Nobel's inventions have become such an accepted part of everyday life that few people realize that these achievements are the result of one person's energy and courage. Instead, the world is reminded once a year of Alfred Nobel's achievements in a completely different context – the presentation of the Nobel Prize. The general public is quite unaware that the prize money involved originally comes from the proceeds of one person's life-work. Most likely, Nobel himself would have found this situation satisfactory. He considered his own achievements to be of little interest for discussion but always appreciated the good work of others.

For many years, the Nobel Prize has been a prestigious, highly respected institution and it gives the impression of being as financially sound as the Bank of Sweden – and equally as boring. Nothing could be further from the truth, however. Alfred Nobel's life, his will, in which he outlines the framework of the prize, the disputed claims to his fortune, all make up a dramatic story, the end of which is still uncertain. This book

9

intends to take a look behind the scenes – providing an insight into what lies behind the ceremony that takes place in Stockholm on December 10th each year with such pomp and circumstance, and what shape the Nobel Prize will take in the future.

The laboratory – a family affair

It is miraculous that Alfred Nobel survived his first years (he was born 1833) considering that he was sickly and frail and that his family was extremely poor for many years. It was due to his mother, Andriette, that he pulled through. She was also one of the few people who really meant something to Nobel.

His father, Immanuel, was an inventor and it was in his laboratories that Alfred received the training in chemistry that became the basis for his inventions. In fact, this was the most beneficial education he received. He only attended a regular school for a few terms between the age of eight and nine before the family moved to Russia. In St Petersburg, the Nobel child received tuition from Swedish and Russian teachers, among others, there was a chemistry professor by the name of Zinin who interested Alfred Nobel in the new substance known as nitro glycerine which the Italian inventor Sobrero had succeeded in producing.

Nitro glycerine was to follow Alfred Nobel throughout his life. But from the beginning it was his father who experimented the most with the substance, first in Russia and later in Sweden. In 1862, Immanuel also successfully demonstrated how nitro glycerine could be manufactured on an industrial basis. During that time, the Nobels and their neighbors lived as if they were on the edge of a volcano ...

Alfred returned to Sweden in order to help his father, while his two older brothers Robert and Ludvig, remained in Russia to sort out their father's complicated business

Alfred Nobel in his laboratory by E. Österman. The painter finished this oil painting after Nobel's death in 1896.

affairs. After Alfred effectively adapted his father's invention, the development was rapid, and one year later he had a patented detonator which used gunpowder to ignite the nitro glycerine. After a further two years, he had developed a detonator cap which made the principle of initial detonation possible – the latter is the basis of all explosives technology to date. In fact this contributed more in the making of a new epoch than all his subsequent inventions – including dynamite.

Like so many other inventions this one had its price, and the Nobel family paid dearly when the entire workshop blew up in an accident which killed Alfred's youngest brother and several others. Shortly afterwards, Nobel senior suffered a stroke and Alfred took over the family business.

Explosive oil – the dream product for the new century

The product the Nobels had succeeded in producing went by the name "explosive oil" and few products have had such enormous marketing potential. Railways were rapidly expanding – not least across the American continent – raw materials needed to be blasted out of the ground to meet the increasing demands from industry, energy requirements mounted and prompted the blasting and excavation of sites for power stations, and the increase in trade required more and better roads. During the first years (i.e. after 1865), Alfred Nobel was the company's managing director, operating engineer, office clerk, salesman, advertising manager and cashier – all at the same time. Even at that stage it wasn't difficult to recognize his incredible capacity for work.

Out of immediate necessity, the company became international. For obvious reasons the explosive oil was extremely dangerous to transport and the need for local manufacture close to the consumers was an essential safety precaution. Further, the product was easy to copy once someone found the formula for the chemical composition of the explosive oil, and local manufacture was one way of protecting the Nobel patent.

The manufacture of explosive oil expanded to Hamburg, Germany and the USA, where factories were quickly set up in California and New York. (The latter was

At the Baku oil fields a range of products were refined at the Nobel works; paraffin (exceeding the total output in the USA), petrol, kerosine, soda and sulphuracid, to mention a few. Technically, the Nobel works under the directorship of Ludvig Nobel were first rate but from a business point of view it took all Alfred's know-how and sound advice to put things right from time to time.

called Atlantic Giant Powder Company, and later became a member of the Du Pont corporation.) The pirated explosive oils which swamped the market caused a great problem, and legal proceedings were initiated in order to protect the original patent. This was not the first time Nobel was forced to take legal action to protect his products. The things that took so much patience and personal risk to experiment on and develop often proved to be all too easy to plagiarize.

Before long, accidents started happening in the handling of explosive oil. Nobel himself insisted that handling instructions should be supplied with each delivery, while the pirate manufacturers were not so careful. Unfortunately it was sometimes also handled like any other oil which meant that some people, for example, tried it out as a lubricant for wagon wheels or as fuel in oil lamps. Needless to say, they only tried these things once.

On the edge of a volcano – safely

It was typical of Alfred Nobel not to sit down and merely express his regrets with each new accident but instead to try and solve the problem in a constructive way. Two years later, in 1867, he presented his new patent which he called "Dynamite". This consisted of three parts nitro glycerine and one part fossil meal (kieselguhr) and, as always when it concerned Nobel, was the result of conscientious research. At last, this product was "safe".

Now, the foundation of what was to

Flash – bang! The 1800's was an "inflammable" century. The explosion that set the stage of the Paris Opera House on fire came at a time when several large theatres had been burned down in the 1870's. The cause was always the same – highly dangerous and insufficient gas lights. Alfred Nobel was just as alarmed as everyone else – the difference was he did something about it. In 1875 he invented a gas burner that was considerably safer. Among other things it pre-heated the air before burning.

become a world-wide industrial empire – in modern terms a multi-national company was formed. Between the years 1871–1873 alone, ten manufacturing plants were started in nine different countries and the speed with which they were established was naturally a result of the fact that dynamite was a vital product in a vital industry. It is important to note that Nobel, contrary to many other inventors, actively participated in the commercial side of launching products and was largely responsible for the formation of companies abroad. He was also a shareholder, usually with a majority holding.

Nobel's years in Paris

In order to be more in the center of what was happening, Alfred Nobel moved to Paris around 1870 and put together a home of sorts on Avenue Malakoff. Here he cultivated his orchids and kept a stable of beautiful carriage horses – it was as close to a hobby as he ever came, if it is at all possible to discuss relaxation when it concerns a person such as Alfred Nobel.

Naturally, there was a laboratory, and although the business and the constant traveling took a great deal of his time, he still continued with his scientific work. Blasting gelatine and Ballestite are two of the products he invented here.

No one can accuse Alfred Nobel of wasting his time on pleasure, even if he lived in Paris – a city always throbbing with activity. Occasionally he was able to arrange dinner parties for selected guests, who were largely colleagues and scientists. And on these occasions he was a considerate host who did his utmost to make his guests feel welcome. There is a moving story from that time about his cook who was leaving her job in order to get married. Nobel told her that he would like to give her a wedding present and wondered if she had anything in mind. She replied that she would like to have as much money as "Mr Nobel earned in one day". An amused Nobel sat down, figured out the amount, and his cook lived on the interest it brought her for the rest of her life.

Although Alfred Nobel said that he regarded business life as a necessary evil and much preferred to spend his time in the world of laboratories, he was still a very ambitious, albeit self-taught, businessman and organizer. At some time during the 1880's he also succeeded in consolidating his various companies into two trusts (the concept was unknown in Europe at this time, only Rockefeller in the USA was engaged in similar transactions)– these trusts were called the English-German trust and the Latin trust respectively. The first world war broke up the organization, but the English trust was later reshaped into what we know today as ICI (Imperial Chemicals Industries Ltd).

Striking oil – in Russia

Unlike Alfred, his older brothers had stayed behind in Russia where the name Nobel had become famous in connection with the great oil discoveries in Baku. It was the eldest brother, Robert, who had promptly staked out a claim in the beginning of the 1870's and he soon had a refinery for the production of paraffin in operation at the site.

A few years later, during a visit to Paris, Robert succeeded in interesting Alfred in the company and together the three brothers founded "Naftaproduktionsbolaget Bröderna Nobel" with head offices in St Petersburg.

The Nobel plants were impressive. The company was responsible for 50% of the

No 53–59 Avenue Malakoff, for nearly 20 years the Paris home of Alfred Nobel. A life long bachelor with an enormous fortune kept only a small house and mixed very little in society. When he entertained guests, mostly engineers and scientists, he was a very gracious host. In this combined home/laboratory more than 50 inventions were patented, among them blasting gelatine and ballestite. It was from here Alfred Nobel created two trusts out of his many companies – a transaction which was completely new to Europe at the time.

In 1879 Alfred Nobel founded the "Branobel" Company (Naftaproduktionsbolaget Bröderna Nobel) together with his two older brothers. The company, with head office in St Petersburg, was a consolidation of the activities already carried out by Robert Nobel at the Baku oil fields in 1870. The three brothers were of an inventive and exploring mind and the refined oil products (mostly paraffin) were transported by pipe lines and cistern trains which they designed themselves. The shipments were carried out by steam-powered tankers which were the first of their kind in the world, another Nobel invention.

NAPHTAPRODUKTIONSGESELLSCHAFT GEBRÜDER NOBEL

ST-PETERSBURG.

EINIGE ABBILDUNGEN DER NAPHTAGEWINNUNG, UND BEARBEITUNG, DER NIEDERLAGEN DER GESELLSCHAFT SOWIE DER FLOTTE FÜR SEE- UND FLUSS-SCHIFFFAHRT.

total production in the area and at the turn of the century the production of the Nobel company alone exceeded the entire paraffin production of the USA. The company had its own gas and electricity works, laboratories, workshops, pipelines and tank trains which carried the products to a harbour on the Caspian Sea for exportation.

The vastness of the Branobel activities in Russia is illustrated by this chart. Every marked place represents an office and/or a depot in the Branobel business network.

The Nobel company provided schools and living accommodations, a steam kitchen and a hospital, parks and a sports stadium for the approximately 7,000 workers and their families. In general, the Nobel brothers exercised a very advanced personnel policy and during Alfred's lifetime, for example, not one strike or lockout ever took place at his companies.

The plants were nationalized in 1918 and, as a result, the part played by the Nobel family in the Russian development of this area came to an end.

A Swedish industrial empire

In 1894, Nobel, who now had two years left to live, bought AB Bofors-Gullspång in Sweden which included an iron works and weapons foundry. This was later complemented with the purchase of the Björneborgs steel mill in order to obtain access to blast furnaces, rolling mill works and the possibilities these gave for the production of steel. Finally, he managed to obtain access to a private energy supply by buying Karåsforsen – all the companies where located within a few miles of each other.

Nobel was now running a neat "little" industry which became the foundation for a large industrial empire which still operates on an international scale. It was Nobel's considered opinion that a country should have a defence industry that was non-reliant on imports from other countries. And when it concerned Sweden's defence, Nobel was an unswerving patriot, exactly as his father Immanuel had been in his time. The fantastic thing about it is that this man, who had meant so much to the foundation of a modern Swedish defence industry, is reported never to have had a Swedish passport (or any other passport for that matter).

Björkborn Manor, near Bofors, which was Nobel's last home in Sweden.

In 1894 Alfred Nobel acquired the iron works and weapons foundry at Bofors and Björkborn, Sweden, in order to continue his experiments with ballestite and artillery applications. First priority was the construction of a modern laboratory at Björkborn which he entrusted to his assistant, Ragnar Sohlman.

The weapons foundry benefited enormously by Nobel's international experience and cosmopolitan outlook not to mention the badly needed capital investment. The engineers and workers saw very little of Mr Nobel who mainly organized the work by letters and telegrams from the capitals of Europe. When in Bofors, he preferred to walk through the empty factories on Sundays as he found his fame was often an obstacle to frank and open technical discussions. He noticed the minutest details and was always keen to suggest improvements. With his international background, he realized that the strength of his new industry was specialization and high quality which became the leading business idea for many years to come.

A surprising will causes a fury

It was an extremely over-worked man who now made the journey between his new home in Sweden and the house in San Remo, Italy. Doctors had diagnosed that, apart from constant chest infections, continual headaches, as well as the beginnings of scurvy, he also suffered from angina pectoris. Alfred Nobel thought that it was an amusing quirk of fate that the medicine he was prescribed for the latter was – nitro glycerine...

In the end, not even his iron will could conquer his worn-out body, and on December the 10th 1896, Alfred Nobel died at his home in San Remo. No friends or relatives managed to reach his death bed in time – he died as lonely as he had lived.

Alfred Nobel, who had so often figured prominently on the front pages of newspapers around the world in connection with his

Alfred Nobel's study in Villa Nobel in San Remo, Italy.

discoveries, accidents, legal disputes over patents, and his success in breaking new ground, caused a sensation yet again when his will and testament was made public. He wanted to leave the largest portion of his enormous fortune to a fund. According to his wishes, the interest on this money would later be given as a financial reward to people who had contributed the most to mankind during the year.

Everyone was in uproar. How could he practically deny the existence of his own family? How should the prize money be administered? How were the prize winners to be chosen? The questions were endless. Was a hand-written will, penned by Alfred Nobel without legal aid – legally binding? Was there any realistic possibility that a Nobel Prize could be created on the basis of such a legally weak document? Today we know the answer – but then, almost 100 years ago, the outcome was highly uncertain.

The laboratory at Villa Nobel, San Remo. One can exaggerate slightly by saying that Alfred Nobel's "home was where he put down his test tubes". Basically a chemist, he never lived far from a laboratory and although a shrewd businessman with interests all over the world, he always returned to his labs. In this private laboratory, he carried out intensive research work between 1891 and 1896, varying from progressive smokeless powder to the making of artificial silk.

View over Côte d'Azur. Here Alfred Nobel found a new home in 1891 after the tumultuous events in Paris and the invention of ballestite. It was also the hope of Alfred Nobel, now in his 60's and completely overworked, that the mild Mediterranean climate would help to cure his chest infections and continual headaches. He first labelled his new home "Mio Nido" (My Nest) but on second thought changed it to Villa Nobel (a "nest" being for a couple, which for an old bachelor was highly inappropriate). It was here Alfred Nobel died on December 10, 1896, of a stroke. Only his Italian servants were present and since he lapsed into his Swedish mother tongue they had no way of understanding his last words. The Villa Nobel is now a very beautiful museum.

LIST OF English PATENTS,

In force, belonging to Mons. Alfred Nobel compiled Dec 4th 1889 with alterations to July 20th 1891

NAME OF PATENTEE	Country	NUMBER AND DATE	TAXES DUE	Subject
H. E. Newton	England	3055 June 28/82 £15 June 28/90	*Expired 1891?*	Cartridges.
"	"	3238 June 29/83 £10 June 29/90	*Expired 1891?*	"
"	"	5382 Mar 24/84 £10 Mar 24/90	*Expired 1891*	Explosive compounds.
"	"	9022 July 27/85 £10 July 27/90	*Expired 1890*	Receptacle for hygroscopic explosives.
"	"	5330 Apr 16/86 £10 Apr 16/90	*Expired 1890*	Explosive compounds.
"	"	5331 Apr 16/86 £10 Apr 16/90	*April 16/92*	" substances.
"	" Wd drop. 92	16656 Dec 18/86 £10 Dec 18/90	*Dec 18/91*	Explosives.
"	"	371 Jan 10/87 £10 Jun 10/91	*Jun 10/92*	Regulating pressure in guns.
"	" 4th drop 92	926 Jun 20/87 £10 Jan 20/91	*Jun 20/92*	Guns + Projectiles.
A. O. Newton	"	3674 Mar 10/87 £10 Mar 10/91	*Expired 1891*	Recoil of Guns.
"	"	5840 Apr 21/87 £10 Apr 21/91	*April 2/92*	Explosive projectiles.
"	"	16919 Dec 8/87 £10 Dec 8/91		Detonator
"	"	16920 Dec 8/87 £10 Dec 8/91		Explosive compounds
"	"	1469 Jan 31/88 £10 Jan 31/92		"
"	"	1470 Jan 31/88 £10 Jan 31/92		Safety Fuses.
"	"	1471 Jan 31/88 £10 Jan 31/92		Explosives.
"	"	6560 May 2/88 £10 May 2/92		Explosive compounds
"	"	10722 July 24/88 £10 July 24/92		"
"	" 6th drop 92	568 Jan 11/89 £10 Jan 11/93		Preventing ignition & retarding combustion.
"	"	1988 Feb 4/89 £10 Feb 4/93		Preparing explosive compounds.
"	"	4479 Mar 14/89 Specification due Dec 14th 1889.	£10 Mar 14/93	Preparation of explosive compounds.
"	"	9361 June 5/89 Ditto Mar 5/90	£10 June 5/93	"
"	"	12307 Aug 2/89 May 2/90	£10 Aug 2/93	Preparation + application of explosive compounds.
"	"	14678 Sept 17/89 June 17/90	£10 Sept 17/93	Cartridges + Guns.

note. All the above are subject to annual Taxes.

The Nobel Prize – the vision emerges

Alfred Nobel's sketchy will was a "hot potato" on a grand scale, and it was no easy task for Ragnar Sohlman and his colleagues to execute a legally valid document. (On the other hand, it is an interesting thought that if the will had been meticulously written in the correct legal style it would probably have been impossible to adapt to contemporary times.)

What, then, was Alfred Nobel trying to achieve with his will? To begin with, his entire fortune was to be invested in "safe papers". The annual interest was to be divided into five parts and given as awards to individuals who had made the most important discoveries or inventions within physics, chemistry, medicine, and within literature to the best author of an ideological work and the so-called peace prize to whoever had worked the most toward achieving the furtherance of international brotherhood, the abolition or reduction of armies, and the organization or propagation of peace congresses.

No consideration whatsoever was to be given to nationality in choosing the prize winners – a typical view by the cosmopolitan Nobel.

The prize givers, one Norwegian and three Swedish institutions, had no prior knowledge of the awesome task given to them by Nobel in his will, and it is understandable that they were doubtful and perplexed over exactly how to proceed. It should also be pointed out that the whole plan involved a vast amount of money – his estate totaled some 33 million Swedish kronor, based on currency values at the turn of the century.

During his lifetime, Alfred Nobel secured around 355 patents – not only from the field of explosives. He once said;
"I'm satisfied if I have 1000 ideas a year and but one proves to be useful".

Alfred Nobel never sought official recognition for himself. In 1893, however, he was made Honorary Doctor at the University of Uppsala, a recognition which pleased him greatly. Twenty-five years earlier he and his father had received a gold medal from the Swedish Academy of Sciences. The award was given for their "findings of the of nitro glycerine and for the invention of dynamite". The Swedish Establishment did not exactly shower its great son with accolades—as the above makes plain. However, the king of Sweden, Oscar II, did honor Alfred Nobel by visiting the scientist's last home, Björkborn, in Sweden. The royal arrival was, of course, saluted with series of explosions!

The battle of the Nobel estate – a legal miracle

The will itself is, in fact, a typical document for Nobel. He drew up the guidelines, appointed good people to do the work and then relied upon them to use their common sense. And the fact that sound judgement was required in order that Nobel's wishes be fulfilled, was completely understood.

After a great deal of in-fighting coupled with clever, high-level diplomacy, Sohlman was the first to succeed in locating the negotiations at Häradsrätten, the district court in the little town of Karlskoga which is the site of Bofors, Nobel's last home.

The next step was to tackle the Nobel relatives. Nobel's nephew in St Petersburg loyally stood by his uncle's last wishes that the fortune should be distributed according to the "Nobel Prize plan". After reaching a compromise, in which the relatives received a little more than they where to have originally received, the job was completed.

Finally, Nobel representatives managed to bring the matter before the Swedish government, where it was established that the government itself (the Crown) would determine the administration and organization of the Prize. In addition, the government had the last word as to the manner in which the prizes would be awarded. The government had no part in choosing the prize winners, however.

Finally – after 3 years' labor – Alfred Nobel's last will and testament was fulfilled. By the year 1900, the rules and regulations for the Nobel Foundation were established and the first five Nobel Prizes were awarded in 1901.

Alfred Nobel's will, in which he states that his fortune was to be turned into a fund and the interest to be given as financial awards – in short the Nobel Prize.

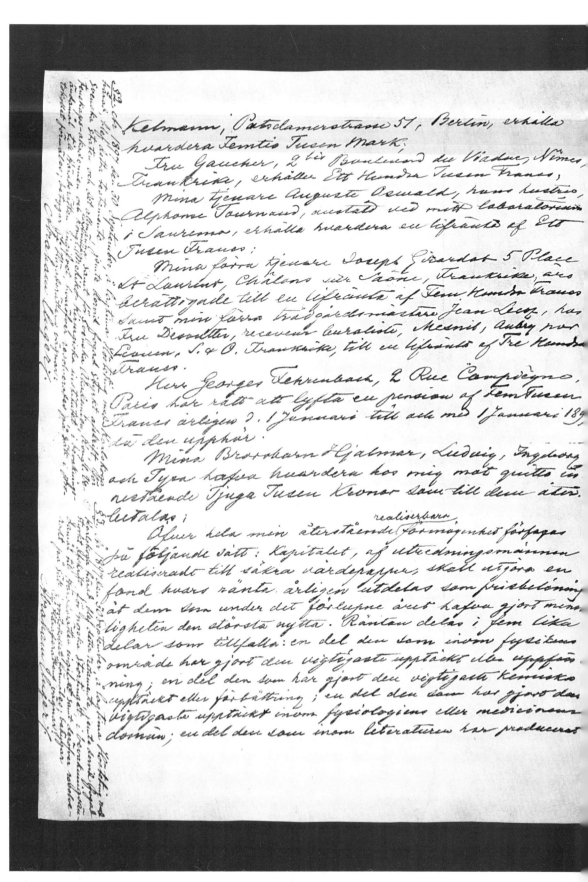

det utmärktaste i idealisk rigtning; och en del åt den
som har verkat mest eller best för folkens förbrödrande
och afskaffande eller minskning af stående armeer
samt bildande och spridande af fredskongresser.
Priset för fysik och kemi utdelas af Svenska Vetenskapsakademien; för fysiologiska eller medicinska
arbeten af Carolinska Institutet i Stockholm; för lite-
ratur af Akademien i Stockholm samt för fredsför-
fäktare af ett utskott af fem personer som väljas
af Norska Stortinget. Det är min uttryckliga
vilja att vid prisutdelningarne intet afseende
fästes vid någon slags nationalitetstillhörighet
sålunda att den värdigaste erhåller priset an-
tingen han är Skandinav eller ej.

Till Exekutorer af dessa mina testamentariska
dispositioner förordnar jag Herr Ragnar Sohlman, bosatt vid Bofors, Vermland, och Herr
Rudolf Lilljequist, 31 Malmskilnadsgatan, Stockholm,
och Bengtsfors i närheten af Uddevalla. Som ersättning
för deras omsorg och besvär tillerkänner jag Herr
Ragnar Sohlman, som antagligen kommer att
egna mesta tid deråt, Ett Hundra Tusen Kronor,
och Herr Rudolf Lilljequist Femtio Tusen Kronor.

Min förmögenhet består för närvarande
dels i fastigheter i Paris och San Remo; dels
i värdepapper förvarande i Union Bank af Scotland
Ld i Glasgow och London; i Crédit Lyonnais,
Comptoir National d'Escompte och hos Alphen, Messin
& Co i Paris; hos fondsmäklaren M.V. Peter & Banque
Transatlantique, afvenledes i Paris; hos Direction
der Disconto Gesellschaft samt Joseph Goldschmidt
& Cie i Berlin; i Ryska Riksbanken samt hos
Herr Emmanuel Nobel i Petersburg; i Skandi-
naviska Kredit Aktiebolaget i Götheborg och Stockholm

The Nobel Prize – hand in hand with the 20th century

Exactly as Nobel had wished, the prizes for physics and chemistry are awarded by the Swedish Academy of Sciences. The prize in Medicine is awarded by the Karolinska Institute and the prize for Literature by the Swedish Academy. The last prize – the Peace Prize – is awarded via the Norwegian Parliament which perhaps sounds a little strange as the other institutions are all Swedish. The reason is quite simply that during Nobel's time the two countries were united.

At present, the Nobel Fund amounts to 360 million Swedish kronor, which in fact, would have been a great deal more if the fund had not been subjected to state income tax during its first 45 years! In addition Nobel's instructions concerning "safe paper" was assumed to mean that the money should be invested in government bonds – and the result was a reduction in the value of the fund due to increasing inflation. In 1953, the obligation to invest in government bonds was abolished and the money was reinvested in other areas so that these losses have now been regained. This means, for example, that the 1982 prize winners shared 1 150 000 Swedish kronor.

The Nobel Foundation has been prompted many times by different interest groups to increase the number of prizes from the original five. It has been suggested that a Nobel Prize be given in music, architecture, mathematics, and the environment to name a few, and donations have been offered simultaneously in order to increase the value of the prizes. If the Nobel Foundation had listened to all the suggestions there would have been by now an "inflation" in Nobel Prizes. One exception has been made, however. In 1968, a sixth Nobel Prize was established in the field of economics. This prize, based on a donation from the National Bank of Sweden, carries the postscript "To the memory of Alfred Nobel" and is awarded by the Swedish Academy of Sciences.

THE NOBEL FOUNDATION

On November the 27th 1895, one year before his solitary death in San Remo, Alfred Nobel put his signature to the four crammed pages that became his last wishes. In doing so, he launched an idea that has made his name more widely known throughout the world today than that of any other living Swede.

From a legal point of view, Nobel's will was a highly dubious document. He donated his large fortune to a non-existent fund and for prizes which where to be awarded by organizations that had never been asked if they were willing to accept the task. But the idea of using extremely large rewards to create recognition for those behind "the greatest services to mankind"; to give awards irrespective of race, religion, or nationality for the promotion of science, literature and peace; all this was an idea that couldn't have been better timed as a new century full of hope for a new golden age of mankind was about to begin.

But this brilliant idea could have been easily extinguished by all the resistance that was raised as soon as the will was made public at the end of December 1896. The countless legal wrangles with dissatisfied and disgruntled members of the family, the hostility of public opinion, the resistance and scepticism of the academies, could have all reduced the will to a beautiful but still-born thought if Nobel had not also nominated an unusual man to act as his executor and trustee. At a time when the voice of youth commanded little respect in the

executor, and the lawyer Carl Lindhagen, Sohlman succeeded after three years of difficult negotiations and decisive action:

1. to get the Nobel will recognized and approved by the entire Nobel family;
2. to convert Nobel's assets and place them in a fund, i.e. to create the Nobel Foundation, according to the instructions in the will;
3. to get the nominated prize givers, the Academy of Sciences, the Karolinska Institute, the Swedish Academy as well as the Norwegian Parliament to accept the undertaking.

The first task was the most difficult and the most sensitive. Alfred Nobel's brother's children felt deeply disappointed at the "modest" inheritance that had been left to them. The Nobels had always been a close family, and they were greatly concerned to see how the sale of their uncle's shareholding in the large Russian oil company owned by the Nobel brothers, as well as those in the explosives companies, would threaten the family's position. However, Sohlman reached an agreement with the Russian branch of the family, led by Nobel's nephew Emanuel, who also became a strong supporter in the struggle to make Alfred Nobel's unusual will a reality. Emanuel Nobel, who was himself exceedingly wealthy, possessed great respect and admiration for his uncle. At one meeting with Sohlman, shortly after the opening of the will, Emanuel remin-

During several dramatic months, this small Swedish courthouse in Karlskoga (near Bofors) held the attention of the world. In this rural setting, Alfred Nobel's will was legally ratified one year after his death. The selection of the site was a fortuitous one for the will's executors, who wisely insisted that Karlskoga was Nobel's last place of residence. Sweden offered the strongest possibility of having the will ratified despite much national criticism directed against Nobel's idea of a prize fund.

venerable professions of older men, Ragnar Sohlman, who was only 26, swept away the apparently insurmountable obstacles within three intensive years, attesting to his almost unbelievable drive and determination. As a result, in June 1900, he was able to witness the establishment of the Nobel Foundation with very large financial resources at its disposal, to be used for five prizes representing services to mankind – all precisely as Nobel had wished.

Those who now study the events during the dramatic years of 1897 – 1900 can only be filled with great admiration and deep respect for Ragnar Sohlman. Like Nobel himself, Sohlman was a chemical engineer and had been employed by Nobel in 1893. He very soon won his employer's utmost confidence during the short time they worked together. A slightly built man, unobtrusive, well mannered and reserved, Sohlman was no superficial heroic type, but it soon became obvious that he possessed the necessary capabilities for the exceedingly difficult tasks involved in realizing Nobel's dreams.

Together with Mr Rudolf Liljeqvist, M. Eng., who was appointed his associate

ded the young engineer who was dreading the tasks ahead, that in Russian the executor of a will was known as the "soul's messenger". Sohlman felt that he personified the wishes of Nobel, and this helped him maintain the strength and resilience with which he tackled his assignment. On behalf of Nobel's worldwide business and industrial interests, Sohlman negotiated with the financial princes and industrial barons of the day, fighting resistance from every quarter – both from King Oscar II and the leader of the social democrats, Hjalmar Branting. He cleverly walked the tightrope between Swedish and Norwegian interests in a situation where the final break-up of the union was becoming increasingly inevitable. He traveled extensively between all the countries and towns where Nobel had interests. On one dramatic occasion, he was forced to carry a loaded revolver to guard a vulnerable shipment of valuables through Paris at night. And in the middle of all this traveling and negotiating he also carried out his military service as Private 114 Sohlman, who was perhaps the most remarkable conscript we have ever had in this country. His telephone calls and telegrams with the capital cities of the world, and not least with the enemies of the Union at Stortinget in Oslo, baffled and upset the officer corps of the king's infantry regiment.

In the summer of 1898, a settlement was finally reached with the Swedish branch of the Nobel family. This partly involved economical concessions to meet the family's demands, and partly an agreement upon the organization and frequency of the Nobel Prize presentations. It was a tough confrontation which engaged many of Europe's most talented lawyers, but the wounds healed quickly, and today the Nobel family is extremely proud of the fact that the world's most prestigious prize bears its name.

Nobel's economic interests were worldwide. The program of divestment, as di-

To convert Nobel's financial resources into a fund was no easy task for the executors of the will. Even after his death patents were still being granted, which is illustrated by this Russian patent granted to the estate in 1901.

rected in the will, was an extremely demanding and difficult one to carry out. The shareholdings in the Nobel dynamite trust, and other subsidiary companies around the world, were relatively easy to dispose of. It was Nobel's personal policy to hold a minority of the shares in his own companies. His authority was based not so much on ownership, but on his technical and financial competence and on the position he naturally assumed as the founder of these companies. His shares in the Russian oil company was a different matter altogether. This particular company's shares suddenly dropped in value on the stock exchange when it became known that one of the largest shareholdings was for sale. After nearly a year of uncertainty, the situation was resolved after Emanuel succeeded in raising the large amount of capital neces-

sary to settle the estate. It was far easier to sell off Nobel's capital investments which were often tied up in high-risk shares in, for example, South African and South American mines and railways.

The most difficult task, however, and the one that took the longest to resolve, was the divestment of Nobel's owner interest in both Bofors and in the Elektrokemiska company in Bengtsfors (Eka). During his short three years as an owner of Bofors, Nobel had invested large amounts in modernizing and developing the company. His strong feelings for the area, and his involvement in the companies, were evident when he made Björkborn Manor in Karlskoga, Bofors, his home – a fact that came to play a decisive role when the courts had to establish the cosmopolitan Nobel's place of residence. The truth was that Nobel had no

official residence and owned no passport which could prove his nationality. In the eyes of the Swedish lawyers, the fact that Nobel had settled in Björkborn made him Swedish. Björkborn also came to be the headquarters for Sohlman's administration and is where the three year dispute over the will was conducted. There was no lack of interest in taking over the ownership of Bofors. Large foreign capital interests were the primary front runners, but Sohlman wanted to keep Bofors in Swedish hands in keeping with Nobel's wishes. A consortium of Swedish companies was finally formed and was able to match the same bid that had been received from abroad.

It took even longer before the Nobel interest in Eka could be disposed of. The company had been started as a joint-venture between Nobel and Liljeqvist and was initially run at a loss. The Nobel Foundation continued to be one of the owners until 1915, when its interests were divested satisfactorily.

Another direct source of revenue from Nobel's activities, which the Nobel Foundation was a recipient of for some time, consisted of royalties and other income from more than 300 Nobel patents. When the resources in the Nobel estate were finally added up they reached 33.2 million Swedish kronor. After settling miscellaneous debts, the net total remained at 31.6 million kronor. The estimated inheritance tax was a total of 3.2 million kronor. After the legacy had been paid and the Nobel family had been satisfied in accordance with the settlement reached in 1898, and after the income

Nobel's first company outside Sweden was founded in Hamburg, Germany. South of the city, in the desolate valley of Krummel, the new company built a factory for the production of nitroglycerine. Many international companies followed suit in Nobel's quickly expanding empire of explosives. At Nobel's death, it was an herculean task to turn his assets into the required Nobel fund.

Sturegatan 14, Stockholm is the heart of the Nobel Foundation. Both the administrative offices for the Foundation and the Nobel Committees for the Royal Swedish Academy of Sciences are located here. The building, acquired in 1916, also includes six private apartments. The day after the ceremony, every Nobel prizewinner steps through the heavy solid doors to pick up the check with the actual prize money.

from the previous three years had been added, the Nobel fortune stood at 31,3 million kronor. This amount then became the initial capital of the Nobel Foundation.

The final and decisive task for Ragnar Sohlman, who was given invaluable help by Carl Lindhagen, later Mayor of Stockholm and a well-known and controversial radical politician, was to persuade the prize awarding institutions to accept their role and become members of the Nobel Foundation. The first one to accept the Nobel offer was the Norwegian Parliament in 1897. The Swedish Academy and the Karolinska Institute followed suit, but not without internal conflict. A positive reply from the Swedish Academy was due largely to the permanent secretary C.D. af Wirsén and was not without stiff resistance from some of the Academy's most influential members. One of these members was the Chief Justice of the Svea Court of Appeal, Hans Forsell, who was also a member of the Academy of Sciences where he managed to organize a resistance movement that was not abandoned until the end of 1898. The Academy of Sciences was an organization very dear to Nobel. He was proud of the fact that he was chosen as a member and in an earlier will had given the Academy the exclusive task of awarding the prizes.

On reflection, it is perhaps not so difficult to understand the hesitation of the designated prize giving organizations. They had never asked to be given this difficult task and were fully aware of the high demands it would place upon them. They also feared the risk of criticism and hostility that such a prize might create.

It is ironic that the institution responsible for the Peace Prize, the most difficult prize to award and the most controversial, was the first to accept, while the Academy of Sciences, which hesitated for a considerable length of time, has won enthusiastic and singular recognition over the presentation of prizes for physics and chemistry.

The Nobel Prize for science provided a new dimension to the activities of the Academy of Sciencies and the Karolinska Institute and has been of immense importance to the development of Swedish research. Even the work of the Swedish Academy came to be strongly affected by its role as a prize giver, and its position as a watchdog of world literature has stimulated and vitalized the entire cultural life of Sweden. The Norwegian Parliament, however, soon found that the role of international prize giver was unsuitable for a national government, and the job was taken over by the Norwegian Nobel Committee whose only link with the Parliament now is that its five members are parliamentary appoint-

Approximately 12 persons are employed at the Nobel Foundation, constantly kept occupied not only with routine administrative work but also with a vast information service. A number of show-cases display artifacts from an extensive donation made by Georg von Békésy, a former Nobel prizewinner (Medicine, 1961). This large and valuable collection, comprised mainly of objects from China and Japan, has been entrusted to the various museums of Stockholm. This collection is by no means the only one to have been bestowed upon the Nobel Foundation over the years. The Foundation has also received the Balzan Prize. Undoubtedly, the largest donation is the one from the Bank of Sweden whose tercentenary foundation endowed the newly created Economics Prize – and together with the Wallenberg Foundation, is the financial source for the Nobel Symposia.

ments. This has extended a greater freedom to the Nobel Committee. The Peace Prize is, for a wider international audience, perhaps the most well-known among all the Nobel Prizes.

1900 – A royal seal of approval for Nobel's dream

On June 29th, 1900, a royal seal of approval was given to the official charter of the Nobel Foundation and Nobel's dreams became a reality. This charter called for a five member board. Three seats were to be appointed by the Swedish Nobel institutions while the positions of chairman and deputy chairman were to be appointed by the Crown. Ragnar Sohlman was an original member of this board until 1946 and served as managing director for the last 17 years. The Norwegian faction declined to appoint a representative to this board but agreed instead to occupy the position of accountant, as well as three seats in the Nobel Foundation's general council which is the foundation's highest supervisory authority. It is interesting to note that the district judge Henrik Santesson, who was the Foundation's first managing director had been the Norwegian Parliament's legal representative during the negotiations to inaugurate the Nobel Foundation. The first chairman was the former prime minister Gustaf Boström, who was re-elected as Prime Minister in 1902 and still remained chairman of the board. Despite the fact that the Foundation is a private one, a strong government influence prevailed which was reflected in the choice of chairmen. Both the prize giving institutions and the Nobel family felt strongly that this kind of authority and prestige would strengthen the fledgling foundation. As the Nobel Foundation and the prizes themselves have received international recognition, the official involvement in the organization has been toned down. The chairman of the board is still appointed by the government but is now selected from among the prize giving organizations.

The Nobel Foundation is responsible for extensive book publication. In addition to Les Prix Nobel which includes the Nobel lectures and biographies of each prizewinner, numerous books have been published on the various Nobel symposia. The plus 50 symposia are the source of books containing purely scientific data as well as books like Science, Technology and Society in Alfred Nobel's Time.

The Nobel Foundation – the conquering of inflation

Today, over 80 years later, it is accurate to say that the Nobel Foundation has become one of the most famous foundations in the world. And yet, from an international perspective, its financial resources are rather limited. During 1982, the assets of the Nobel Foundation were worth approximately 450 million kronor which could be compared with the large American foundations whose assets are in billions. It is primarily through its total commitment to *one* task, awarding the prizes, that the Foundation has achieved its unique position.

Since the beginning, the main objective of the Nobel Foundation has been to administer the Nobel inheritance and to ensure that the Nobel Prize winners, according to its patrons wishes, should receive a substantial prize. By securing a strong economic base for the work of the prize institutions the Nobel Foundation is able to guarantee absolute independence and freedom from outside interests and influence. This is only one of the reasons responsible for the continual high regard for the Nobel Prize.

The initial capital of 31.3 million kronor has been converted into 450 million, but would have been twice that amount had the Foundation not been so highly taxed during its first 50 years. Because the Foundation's investment possibilities at the turn of the century were limited strictly to government bonds, it was quite vulnerable to the massive inflation which raged during the first and second World Wars. In 1901, a Nobel prizewinner received 150,000 kronor, the equivalent of a professor's earnings over 25 years. By the 1950's, the value of the prize had decreased by two thirds. After paying roughly 15 million kronor to the state government since 1900, the Foundation was made exempt from state income tax in 1946. The Foundation continues to pay, however, a large number of other state and local government taxes and levies (in 1981 these amounted to about 3 million kronor). At the risk of its capital completely melting away, the Foundation was relieved of its old obligation to invest in government bonds in

The Nobel Prize's
development since 1901*

PRIZE AMOUNTS

year	in Swedish kronor
1901	150.800
1910	140.700
1920	134.100
1923	115.000
1930	172.900
1940	138.600
1950	164.500
1960	226.000
1970	400.000
1971	450.000
1972	480.000
1973	510.000
1974	550.000
1975	630.000
1976	681.000
1977	700.000
1978	725.000
1979	800.000
1980	880.000
1981	1.000.000
1982	1.150.000
1983	1.500.000

The prize money is taxed in accordance with the laws of the country of the recipient. As a rule the prize is tax free either *de jure* or *de facto*.

The Nobel Prize's
Nominal Amount

1953 Value of
the Nobel Prize

The Nobel Prize
at 1901 price level

1901   1920   1940   1960   1980 81 82

Figures given in Swedish Kronor

2 000 000
1 800 000
1 600 000
1 400 000
1 200 000
1 000 000
800 000
600 000
400 000
200 000

1953 and was then free to invest its resources in whatever offered the best possible financial return so that the value of the prize could be easily increased.

During the last 30 years this opportunity to invest freely has led to the recovery of lost capital and the value of the Nobel Prize has successively climbed – both nominally and in real terms. The 1983 prizes now stand at 1 500 000 kronor. The economic administration of the Nobel Prize is now largely managed as if the Foundation were an investment company. The Nobel capital of 450 million Swedish kronor is invested in property, stocks and shares and other investments that yield interest. About 15% of the Foundation's resources are invested abroad.

One new prize has been added to the list: "the Alfred Nobel Memorial Prize in Economic Sciences", which was initiated in 1968. This prize is endorsed by the Bank of Sweden, and is awarded by the Academy of Sciences. The donation from the bank was made as a gesture to celebrate the bank's 300th anniversary.

The Economics Prize is the exception that confirms the rules – no new Nobel Prizes beyond the five prizes stipulated by Nobel himself in his will, directly reflective of his own interests and activities. Each year, the Nobel Foundation receives many recommendations for new prizes, often supported by promises of large donations. These include prizes for mathematics, astronomy, music, the protection of the environment, and architecture, to name only a few. Needless to say, the Foundation has rejected all these proposals. An inflation in Nobel Prizes would be created with each new addition and the value of the original prizes would diminish.

A once quiet affair – now a festival for millions

The international success of the Nobel Prize has meant a voluminous, world wide correspondance for the Foundation.

Letters and enquiries pour in constantly every day. Representatives of foreign press, radio and television are frequent guests at the Nobel House. The internatio-

The Nobel banquet is given at the Town Hall on the evening of the 10th of December in the presence of the royal family. The dining hall takes 1310 seated guests and the demand for invitations and dinner tickers is enormous.

nal interest culminates each year in the Nobel Prize ceremony on December 10th, a ceremony that has grown into a Nobel week, or "the Nobel Festival" as it is called outside Sweden. What was a relatively quiet affair over 80 years ago, involving about 100 guests, has now become a festival with thousands of participants. More than 1 300 guests attended the 1981 Nobel Banquet held at the Stockholm Town Hall. In addition, millions of people follow the festivities through direct radio and television broadcasts. Since 1901, the prizes have always been presented in Stockholm by the king or the crown prince, and in Oslo by the chairman of the Peace Prize Committee in the presence of the Norwegian royal family.

In recent years, a new aspect the week's events is the appearance of Nobel symposiums. The Foundation has been responsible for more than 50 scientific symposiums since 1968. The Nobel symposiums are organized in cooperation with the Nobel Committees. About 40 highly qualified scientists and scholars are invited to a 3–4 day symposium dealing with current major research developments or a relevant multidisciplinary subject. At least two thirds of the participants must be non-Scandinavians. The lectures and the discussions given at the symposiums are later published in book form by an international publisher.

Endowing a vital force

The symposiums were initially sponsored by the Bank of Sweden tercentenary foundation. Beginning in 1983 they will be financed by a grant from the Nobel Foundation's symposium fund of 6 million kronor, supplemented by donations from the Anniversary Fund and the Knut and Alice Wallenberg Foundation. The Nobel Foundation itself contributes with a certain amount of income from royalties.

Over the years the Nobel Foundation has received numerous donations. In 1962, the Foundation received the Balzan prize consisting of one million swiss francs. Ten years later, the Foundation became the sole inheritor of Georg von Békésy's exceedingly valuable collection of Asian art and antiques. The Foundation has bestowed the collection among museums in Stockholm, predominantly the Museum of Far Eastern Antiquities. In that same year, the Foundation also inherited two wine chateaus near Tarranto in Italy, donated by the marquis of Beaumont-Bonelli. The property has since been sold and the proceeds, 4 million kronor, have been placed in a fund whose interest is used to finance the Nobel Foundation's international activities. For example, a young Italian scientist is given an annual scholarship enabling him or her to work at the Karolinska Institute in Stockholm. In this way, the success of the Nobel prizes have resulted in new donations totaling approximately 10 million kronor for the benefit and furtherance of international scientific and cultural cooperation.

The Nobel Foundation represents the Nobel inheritance and its intentions as specified in Alfred Nobel's will. In other words, it continues to carry out in Sohlman's role as "the soul's messenger". The Foundation supports and finances the prizes, but the responsibility for chosing the prize winners lies entirely with the prize giving institutions. During the past 80 years, these institutions which originally accepted their task with considerable hesitation, have carried out their work with impartiality, competence and devotion. It is thanks to the efforts of these institutions that it has been possible for Alfred Nobel's foundation to become a vital force in the world's scientific and cultural development.

In 1968, the Nobel Foundation initiated a new event – the Nobel Symposia. These scientific symposia, largely financed by the Bank of Sweden tercentenary foundation, are organized by the Foundation in cooperation with the Nobel Committees. This particular symposium, held in 1981, was on the theme of "Science, Technology and Society in Alfred Nobel's Time" and the location was none other than Nobel's last home – the Björkborn Manor in central Sweden.

This little ceramic figure is from Georg von Békésy's collection, bequeathed to the Foundation in 1972. The figure which dates back to the Ming Dynasty (1368–1644), now guards one of the hallways in the Nobel House from "evil spirits".

THE SELECTION OF A NOBEL PRIZE WINNER

... *"I wish to convey to you our warmest congratulations and now ask you to receive the prize from the hands of his Majesty the King."*

Upon hearing these words, repeated each year since 1901, Nobel prizewinners stand up, go forward to the King of Sweden and receive a solid gold medal and a diploma. But of all the writers and scientists in the world, how did she or he come to be standing there in Stockholm's Concert House?

At times, the occasion of the Nobel awards seems to provide a greater opportunity to criticize the choice rather than to acknowledge a winner.

Naturally, Nobel's prestigious prize is bound to provoke controversy. It always has and undoubtedly always will. The announcement makes international headlines and names that had been obscure an hour earlier are transformed suddenly into first class interviewing subjects – scientific work is spotlighted and discussed.

"(The Nobel Prize) is very good from the point of view that it advertises the field. It gets announced and people get aware of the fact that there are physicists around, or chemists or doctors. The Prize is front page news."
/Interview Nobel prizewinner/

Inevitably, there is much pre-announcement speculation about "who is going to get it this year". Speculation for the scientific prizes usually circulates in small groups,

whereas the prize winners in Literature and Peace are almost announced in the press before the award committees get a chance to sit down and make a decision.

The speculation may be expansive and the criticism thick but one is astonished to discover how much is said with no idea of HOW A NOBEL PRIZEWINNER IS ACTUALLY CHOSEN. Indeed, many prizewinners themselves have a rather vague notion of how they were chosen.

It All Goes Back to the Will

Every aspect of the Nobel Prize has its origin in Alfred Nobel's will. This handwritten document, dated 1895, determines the financial means for the prize, for what the prize is awarded and who is to be responsible for these awards. The general terms and phrasing of the will caused initial confusion, resulting in misconceptions which would have been greater had not the executors proved to be so visionary and the awarding institutions so conscientious in embracing their new responsibility.

After expeditious work – by legal standards – the Swedish Nobel Prize establishment was ready to begin its work by 1900–1901. By then the statutes had been drawn up and given authority by the King in Council. In December 1901, the first Nobel prizewinners, among them Röntgen, von Behring and Henri Dunant, received their awards. The Nobel Prize and the 20th century have accompanied each other.

How were they selected? And would they be chosen by today's standards? In short – has the procedure changed in over

The 18 members of the Swedish Academy at one of their Thursday meetings. During these regular weekly work sessions, the members keep each other continuously informed about the incoming nominations for the year's Nobel prizewinner. At least 12 members must be present when the decision is made. This vote is preceded by long hours of discussion through the months.

80 years? The answer is: perhaps. There are some changes from the original procedures – occurring mainly within the other keystone of the Nobel Prize – the nominations.

The Decision

Intense criticism unleashes as soon as the announcement is made, yet very few realize the hundreds of candidates nominated by, in some cases, thousands of individuals. The winner represents only the tip of a very large and resolute iceberg. For instance, in Medicine, behind a group of 50 persons who decide, there are roughly 3,000 individuals from all over the world who are asked to name a candidate each year.

"The Prize Committee has done pretty well. They do not miss anybody who is extremely important."
/Interview Nobel prizewinner/

The "Big Four" prize awarding institutions work independently of each other when they select their winners, but the nomination procedure is very much the same for each. The laureate in Literature has been through the same intense scrutiny as have the laureates in Physics, Medicine or Peace. With more than 80 years' experience, the four institutions have become extremely discerning in their choice of a winner.

These institutions were selected by Alfred Nobel without their knowledge. Little did they anticipate the way in which

they would be propelled from Scandinavia, into a world community. With the exception of one, the Norwegian parliament which was to award the Peace Prize – the three academies had their roots in Swedish cultural and scientific life. After a great deal of deliberation, they accepted these new responsibilities and actively sought a greater international perspective while simultaneously carrying out their ordinary duties.

It is often said that the life of a Nobel prizewinner is never the same. This may also be said for the prize awarding institutions. Take the *Swedish Academy*, for example. It had cultivated and stimulated Swedish literature and the Swedish language since 1783.

Now, its 18 members read more world literature than anything else and have at

The Awarding Organisations

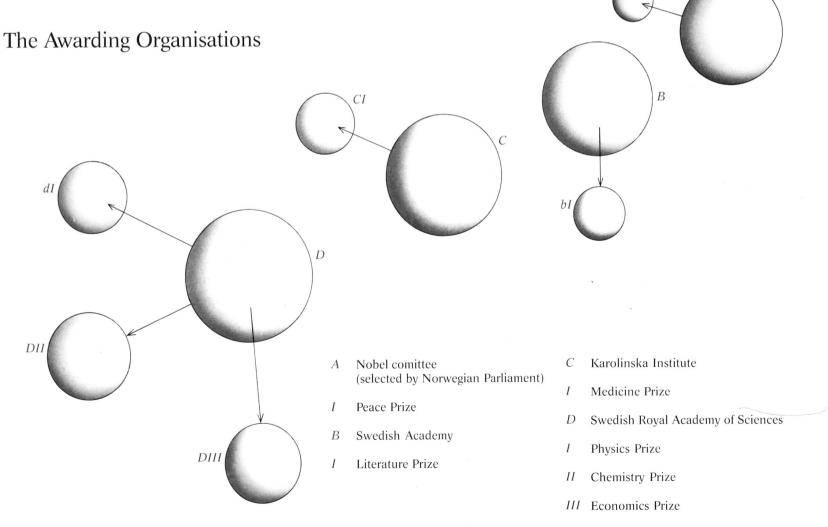

A	Nobel comittee (selected by Norwegian Parliament)	C	Karolinska Institute
I	Peace Prize	I	Medicine Prize
B	Swedish Academy	D	Swedish Royal Academy of Sciences
I	Literature Prize	I	Physics Prize
		II	Chemistry Prize
		III	Economics Prize

Nomination and Selection of Nobel Prize Winners

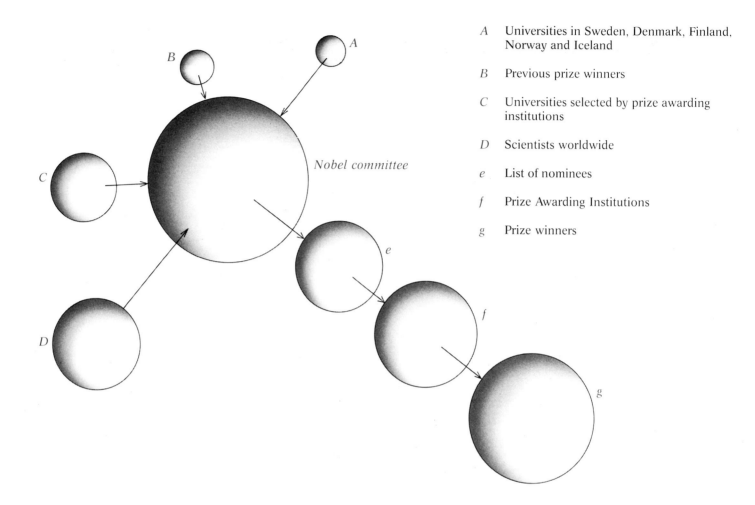

A   Universities in Sweden, Denmark, Finland, Norway and Iceland

B   Previous prize winners

C   Universities selected by prize awarding institutions

D   Scientists worldwide

e   List of nominees

f   Prize Awarding Institutions

g   Prize winners

their disposal a library holding three kilometers of shelves for just these books.

The *Karolinska Institute* was involved, through indirectly, before the will was ever written. Nobel's addendum, which specified that there be a single prize for both medicine and physiology was due to the influence of Dr. Jöns Johansson of the Institute who had also worked in Nobel's laboratory in Paris. Johansson told Nobel about the progress in this field of science, quite unaware of the effect it had on him until the appearance of the will. Behaviorist Konrad Lorenz, the 1974 winner, certainly embodied this fusion of the two fields.

The *Royal Swedish Academy of Sciences* decides upon three prizes: Physics, Chemistry and since 1968, Economics, a field not included in the original will. The Bank of Sweden initiated and endowed the Alfred Nobel memorial Prize in Economic Sciences in commemoration of their 300th anniversary. With its 385 members, the Royal Academy of Sciences is the largest of the Nobel Institutions, while the Peace Prize is awarded by the smallest of the institutions, consisting of five members.

The five persons who comprise the *Norwegian Nobel Committee* have the Herculean task of finding a champion of peace in a world which constantly hovers on the precipice of world war. The Committee receives fierce criticism no matter how they interpret Alfred Nobel's words: "The prize should be awarded the person who shall have done the most or the best work for fraternity between nations, for the abolition or redcution of standing armies and for the holding and promotion of peace congresses." An extensive statement, to say the least.

Why was a Norwegian institution included in an otherwise Swedish affair? At the time of the will, Sweden and Norway had formed a consolidated union, much like that of Scotland and England. When this alliance was dissolved in 1905, it did not affect the Nobel Institution which by then had acquired a thriving life of its own.

The Aura

"The Nobel Prize represents a unique value in that it is recognized as the outstanding prize in science. I think that its psychological value is important to the people of the world, the appreciation of the fact that science is for the people."
/Interview, Nobel prizewinner/

Over the years, there have been countless heated discussions about the appropriateness of some small institutions in a remote country like Sweden conveying the world's highest honor upon international scientific and literary achievement.

Undeniably, both Alfred Nobel and the prize he envisioned are Swedish. Nobel created something that the world was quite hungry for: a prize "… that the most worthy shall receive, whether he be a Scandinavian or not". But the making of the Nobel prize, the arduous realization of Nobel's intentions, *is* a Swedish endeavour. The institutions named by Nobel have enacted their responsibilities wholeheartedly, infusing the prize with respect and awe. Thanks to their efforts, Sweden has turned fully toward the world and the world has responded by turning to Sweden.

The Nominations: A Crucial process

A Nobel prize worth only a nominal sum of money would, quite frankly, not be so attractive to either the winners or the public. Further, a desultory nomination procedure would be equally disastrous. So, endless care is taken to maintain a multifarious and thorough nominating process.

The originally designed nominating procedure still endures.

Every year approximately two to three thousand individuals, *per prize group*, are invited to suggest candidates for the Nobel Prize. These range from Universities in Africa to Pen Clubs in the USSR, from scientists in Malaysia to Egyptian professors.

Former Nobel prizewinners are always included on the list. They tend to be actively involved for several years after winning their own award – but later on their commitment diminishes. Interestingly enough, former winners of the prize in medicine are more active than the winners of any other prize group and decidedly more international in scope when naming candidates.

Five Small and Important Committees

All suggestions must be submitted in writing to the appropriate Nobel Committee and supplemented with printed works verifying the candidates' qualifications for the prize. Each Committee, numbering five persons, also has the right to propose candidates. The potential weight of these particular nominations varies among the Committees. In Physics, for instance, Committee members rarely add their own proposals to the existing list of candidates.

The most participatory Nobel Committees are, in fact, those for Literature and Peace; especially the latter, since it both suggests and decides upon who receives the prize. The Committee in Literature frequently adds names to the 300–400 suggestions which come in each year from around the world. Because some of these are for the same writer, the list actually covers about 100–150 names.

The announcement of this year's Nobel laureates in Chemistry, Physics and Economy is made at the Royal Academy of Sciences. As usual, the event is given extensive coverage by the media.

K·KAROLINSKA
MEDIKO-KIRURGISKA
INSTITUTET

vilket enligt testamente / som den 27
November 1895 upprättats

af

ALFRED NOBEL

eger att med NOBEL- pris belöna den Viktigaste upptäckt / hvar-
med de fysiologiska och medicinska
vetenskaperna under senaste tiden
riktats / har denna dag beslutit att till-
erkänna det år 1901 utgående priset

ät
EMIL von B

för hans arbete rörande
och särskildt dell anvä
hvarigenom han brutit
den medicinska veten
gifvit läkaren ett seg
pal mot sjukdom o
Stockholm de
Karolinsk
mediko — kirurgist
Lärarekoll

HRING

...mterapien
...g mot difteri
...väg inom
...s område och
...vapen i kam-
...d.

...Okt. 1901.

...nstitutets

...

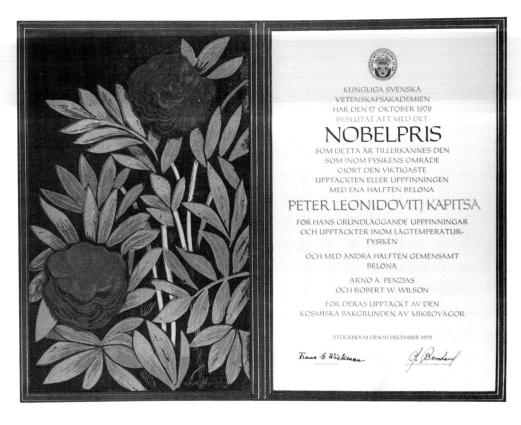

KUNGLIGA SVENSKA
VETENSKAPSAKADEMIEN
HAR DEN 17 OKTOBER 1978
BESLUTAT ATT MED DET

NOBELPRIS

SOM DETTA ÅR TILLERKÄNNES DEN
SOM INOM FYSIKENS OMRÅDE
GJORT DEN VIKTIGASTE
UPPTÄCKTEN ELLER UPPFINNINGEN
MED ENA HÄLFTEN BELÖNA

PETER LEONIDOVITJ KAPITSA

FÖR HANS GRUNDLÄGGANDE UPPFINNINGAR
OCH UPPTÄCKTER INOM LÅGTEMPERATUR-
FYSIKEN

OCH MED ANDRA HÄLFTEN GEMENSAMT
BELÖNA

ARNO A. PENZIAS
OCH ROBERT W. WILSON

FÖR DERAS UPPTÄCKT AV DEN
KOSMISKA BAKGRUNDEN AV MIKROVÅGOR

STOCKHOLM DEN 10 DECEMBER 1978

KUNGLIGA SVENSKA
VETENSKAPSAKADEMIEN
HAR DEN 16 OKTOBER 1978
BESLUTAT UTDELA DET AV
SVERIGES RIKSBANK
ÅR 1968 INSTIFTADE PRISET
I EKONOMISK VETENSKAP TILL

ALFRED NOBELS MINNE

TILL

HERBERT A. SIMON

FÖR HANS BANBRYTANDE FORSKNING
OM BESLUTSPROCESSEN INOM
EKONOMISKA ORGANISATIONER

STOCKHOLM DEN 10 DECEMBER 1978

The Literature Committee reads and monitors a gret deal of what is published in world literature. New "faces" appear each year though in all certainty, a candidate's name will reappear on the list for several years. It would be extremely unusual to receive the prize in the same year one's name first rises to the list.

A Strong Scandinavian Influence

Patriotism was an intense force at the turn of the century. By stressing the irrelevancy of nationality, Alfred Nobel brought a new dimension to an already sophisticated prize concept. The first step towards internationalism was the inclusion of professors at the universities in Denmark, Norway, Finland and Iceland, and vesting them with the right to nominate.

In the early decades, every one of these professors would receive a personal letter from the Nobel Committee with an invitation to submit their nominations. No longer – expediency has replaced decorum, of necessity. Now, it is the deans and provosts of these Nordic universities who receive a yearly reminder of their rights with nomination forms enclosed. Surprisingly, very few of them are returned.

This partial lack of response is offset by the many proposals frequently turned in to the Literature Committee by Swedish and Norwegian professors. Thus the Scandinavian influence on the Nobel Prize has remained strong from the beginning.

An Invitation to the World

If a country would like to organize a campaign to launch a particular candidate, nothing could be easier. In order to obtain extensive geographical coverage, the prize committee statutes state that professors "or holdes of corresponding chairs in at least six universities" worldwide are to be invited to submit proposals. Certain universities are included every year – with a wide range of other universities approached intermittently.

Take for example the Nobel Committee for Physics. Professors and scientists in the countries of France, the United States, West Germany, Italy, Soviet Union, the Netherlands, Belgium and Switzerland always receive annual invitations from this Committee.

The Nobel Prize in Medicine concentrates on members of about ten medical faculties, with some 40 nominators alternated every year to ensure good geographical coverage. This effort seems to yield satisfying results from the nominators in Medicine. Those in Physics and Chemistry apply other procedures and techniques. As one can clearly see, distinctive personalities have emerged from each one of the Nobel Committees.

At any rate, this campaign effort is unusual and seldom initiated – though not unknown in literature – particularly from minority languages such as Basque and Gaelic. But minority languages have been reflected with these winners: the Indian poet Rabindranath Tagore (1913) wrote both in English and his native Bengali, Frédéric Mistral (1904) wrote in Provençal, and Isaac Bashevis Singer (1978) still tells his stories in Yiddish. Especially since World War II, the Nobel Prize has conferred a unique sense of national, regional and ethnic integrity.

The Nobel Library stores its valuables in safe deposit boxes in Börshuset's (The Stock Exchange) renovated cellar.

The Swedish Academy shares office suites with the Stock Exchange in Stockholm's old city. This beautiful building which dates back to the 18th century, is the perfect setting for the Nobel Foundation's annual reception for the prizewinners. The grand occasion is held on the evening prior to the prize presentation.

The Scientific Community Converges

By right of the statutes, the last category of persons who may propose Nobel prize-winners is individual scientists – by invitation only, of course.

Because a Nobel prizewinner in Chemistry might just as easily have received it for discoveries in Medicine, the Nobel Committee seeks to ensure maximal freedom for each prize institution to consider opinions of all scientists regardless of their field of research. By freely engaging a wide range of scientific thought, the work of the Prize Committees is simultaneously clarified and increased. In Physics, the result of this quest is a total of 60 to 70 new candidates.

And what about the prize awarding institutions themselves? Do they literally just pick one name from the list? Hardly. The assiduously prepared nomination lists are a constellate of the best there is to decide upon. However, a few Nobel prizewinners *have* been chosen without their names first appearing on any list.

Behind Closed Doors

After the extensive nomination procedure, the institutions retire for the exclusive purpose of discussion and an ultimate decision. Whatever happens behind closed doors at the Swedish Academy, the Royal Academy

The Bank of Sweden has effected the only change in Nobel's original stipulation that there be five Prizes. In 1968, the Bank celebrated its 300th anniversary with a donation to the Nobel Foundation thus establishing a sixth prize, in Economics, dedicated to the memory of Alfred Nobel. The Royal Swedish Academy of Sciences awards the Economics Prize in strict keeping with the nomination procedure for the prizes in Chemistry and Physics. The first Prize, awarded in 1969, was monetarily commensurate with the other Prizes.

of Sciences, the Nobel Assembly of the Karolinska Institute and the Nobel Committee in Norway is rarely revealed, and only after 50 years.

The doors open one day in late October, someone emerges, cameras flash, and a statement is read announcing the year's Nobel prizewinners. The questions resound: Was the choice unanimous? Why not X? Was Professor X close to getting it? Silence is the only answer. The solitary thing that will be revealed on this day is the final decision.

Such a secretive atmosphere breeds speculation, though sometimes, notably in Literature, these speculations are surprisingly accurate. There is a story that the Permanent Secretary of the Swedish Academy asked the journalists why they were waiting for something as anti-climactical as the official announcement. Without a doubt, many publishing houses would like to get a reliable prediction beforehand ...

The Nobel Calendar

By the early autumn of 1985, invitational letters will be distributed for 1986's candidates, precisely on schedule. The deadline for their return is January 31st. The decision is made before November 15th, and the prizes are awarded on December 10th.

Before the prizewinners begin their dessert at the Nobel Banquet, the nomina-

Certainly each of the five secretaries of the Nobel Committees are committed to their considerable responsibilities but it is Lars Gyllensten who receives all of the attention. As permanent secretary of the Swedish Academy, Mr. Gyllensten has the pleasure of announcing the winner of the Literature Prize. He himself is a prominent author with inexhustible patience when asked to explain the selection process of prizewinners according to Nobel's will. One Thursday in October, he will emerge from his office and name the year's Nobel prizewinner in Literature.

tion period for next year's candidates is in full swing, orbiting in a cycle more regular than the seasons. Will there always be a Nobel Prize? As long as the nominations continue to come in and the prize money steadily increases, the Nobel Prize has an excellent chance of reaching its centenary.

The Future

The future of the Nobel prize is difficult to gauge when so little is known about the decision process itself. One can only closely monitor the prevailing winds and speculate wisely.

In Literature, philosophers like Bertrand Russel (1950) and Henri Bergson (1927) or historians such as Winston Churchill (1953) were singular award winners, never to be repeated. Now, only poets, novelists in fiction and playwrights may be taken into consideration.

The inclination to award a Nobel Prize on the basis of a single work went out of practice with Hemmingway's *The Old Man and the Sea*. The Academy now prefers to regard a writer's total production or the wholeness of a life's work – with respect to its influence on the traditions from which it sprang, as for example, W. B. Yeats' Ireland, Gabriella Mistral's Chile or Giorgos Seferis' Greece.

Third World writers will certainly become more prominent in the future, though these authors are haunted by a lack of access to publication. The Swedish Academy is certainly aware of this grave inadequacy. Like a composer without an orchestra, a writer remains unheard unless published.

A Shared Prize

The tendency of the Physics Prize to be shared among two, sometimes three winners is hardly a policy of the prize institution. It simply reflects the preponderance of collaborative research projects. In Theoretical Physics, it is quite usual for more than one person to take part in a breakthrough, and by Nobel standards, these scientists, like athletes in their prime, are exceptionally young.

Despite increasing difficulty in doing so, the Royal Academy defies the propensity toward a shared prize in Chemistry and strives to uphold a policy of one prize – one winner.

The early prizes in Medicine were awarded primarily for cures in tropical diseases. In 1901, von Behring's serum against diphteria was described as having "placed in the hands of the physician a victorious weapon against illness and deaths". Medical discoveries have taken their own quantum leap. The 1980 prize acknowledged the joint discovery of genetically determined codes inscribed on cell surfaces which regulate immunological reactions.

Discoveries continue to flood in at an unprecedented speed. But no matter how many major discoveries are made "during the past year", as Alfred Nobel wrote, there are only five Nobel Prizes to be awarded each year. This finite number fails to discourage those scientists whose contributions and discoveries will not win a Nobel Prize. And their research, Alfred Nobel would assuredly agree, is a great thing, vital and necessary to us all.

The announcement of the Nobel prizewinners in Medicine. Sometime during the late fall (deadline is November 15th), the awarding institutions must decide on "who will get it" and the press eagerly awaits the result. Within minutes, the news is dispatched and a handful of men and possibly women will find their names linked from now on with the Nobel Prize. It is a formal policy that nothing be revealed of the sometimes heated discussions which precede the announcement. The awarding institutions have agreed to make some of the material public after 50 years, provided that the prizewinners in question are deceased.

The Concert Hall in Stockholm where the Nobel prizes are presented by the King of Sweden on the 10th of December each year.

A NOBEL PRIZE WINNER IN STOCKHOLM

On October 19th, 1981 Professor Kenichi Fukui received a telegram informing him that he had been awarded that year's Nobel Prize for chemistry. The telegram was from the Royal Swedish Academy of Sciences which informs the winners, either by telephone or telegram, of their awards as the announcements are made. At the same time the news is released to the press. As the nominations for the Nobel Prize are always kept secret, Professor Fukui was extremely surprised and happy, and the congratulations soon began to pour in.

Already a well known scientist in Japan, Professor Fukui's prize becomes a national event once the telegram is sent from Sweden. The first letter of congratulations arrives from the Imperial Court and includes an invitation for lunch. This provides an opportunity for the Emperor to give his congratulations personally.

Professor Fukui also received the customary official invitation to Stockholm. An earlier visit to the Swedish University in Uppsala was very much like a routine business trip. The one ahead of him now as a newly announced Nobel prizewinner will be markedly different. A flock of Japanese journalists will make sure of that. From this moment, Professor Fukui's every step is recorded.

After weeks of intensive planning Professor Fukui, together with his wife Tomoe and his associate, Professor Tokio Yamabe boarded a plane on December 5th bound for Sweden. The Nobel week had begun . . .

```
TELEGRAM

1981-10-19

PROFESSOR KENICHI FUKUI
DEPARTMENT OF HYDROCARBON CHEMISTRY
FACULTY OF ENGINEERING
KYOTO UNIVERSITY
KYOTO, JAPAN


DEAR PROFESSOR FUKUI,

I HAVE THE PLEASURE TO INFORM YOU THAT THE ROYAL SWEDISH
ACADEMY OF SCIENCES TODAY HAS DECIDED TO AWARD THE
1981 YEAR'S NOBEL PRIZE IN CHEMISTRY TO BE SHARED BY YOU
AND PROFESSOR ROALD HOFFMANN, CORNELL UNIVERSITY FOR YOUR
THEORIES, DEVELOPED INDEPENDENTLY, CONCERNING THE COURSE
OF CHEMICAL REACTIONS.


TORD GANELIUS
SECRETARY GENERAL
```

On arrival in Stockholm, a limousine, and an official from the Swedish Foreign Office assigned to be Professor Fukui's personal assistant during his visit in Sweden, are waiting. The official, Mr. Stellan Ottosson, will assist with the hectic arrangements that await the Nobel Prize winner and is naturally honoured to have been given the assignment.

Professor Fukui quickly becomes of great interest to the press, which is often the case when a Nobel Prize winner comes from a non-European country. Everyone knows that he was born on October 4, 1918; that he took his doctor's degree at the Kyoto University in 1948 and works in the university's Department of Hydrocarbon Chemistry, and that he has been a full professor since 1951. Beyond these few facts, the mass media attempts to obtain more personal details of the man himself, as it is often difficult to present complex scientific research to a wide audience. During their stay in Stockholm, the Nobel Prize winners are required to answer innumerable questions from journalists who have come from all over the world. Many of the questions are purely scientific, some are personal. But from this moment on, and for the rest of his professional life, Professor Fukui will be asked to give his views on a wide variety of different subjects. For a Nobel Prize winner is considered to know everything, or at least to be able to have an answer for everything. Here the prize winners for chemistry and physics meet the press at the Academy of Sciences a few days before the official presentation.

According to the charter of the Nobel Fund, prize winners have only one obligation—to give a Nobel lecture. These days, this takes place on December 8 and preparations are made for the speeches from the moment the prize winners are announced in October. On the same day, but in different lecture theatres in Stockholm, the 1981 Nobel Prize winners give their speeches.

As the Royal Swedish Academy of Sciences awards the Nobel Prize for chemistry, Professor Fukui gives his Nobel lecture on the Role of Frontier Orbitals in Chemical Reactions, in the academy's lecture theatre. Professor Hoffman, who shares the prize, as well as the award winner for Physics, also gives his speech at the same academy.

On December 9th, the day before the official presentations, it is the Nobel Foundation's turn to stage a reception for the prize winners and their guests. The reception is held in the main hall of the Stockholm Stock Exchange. It is a beautiful building lying adjacent to the Royal Palace and since 1863 has housed the Stockholm Stock Exchange. Another part of this building is occupied by the Swedish Academy responsible for awarding the Nobel Prize for Literature.

The great day has arrived. According to tradition the Nobel Prizes are presented on December 10th in the Stockholm Concert Hall. Att the Nobel Prize winners have been rehearsing the program here since 11 a.m. to ensure that nothing goes wrong and disturbs the auspicious occasion. Everyone has been told where they are to sit, walk, and stand. Ever since the first Nobel Prize presentation in 1901, the awards have been personally presented by the King of Sweden. The present king, Karl XVI Gustav, has inherited the role from his grandfather. Through the years this has been a duty welcomed by the Swedish king and he feels as honored as the prize winners on this occasion. During the prize giving ceremony, the organizers have tried to include a ceremony which in different ways is associated both with Nobel and with the prize winners themselves. All the flowers that decorate the Concert Hall have been donated by the town of San Remo (where Nobel lived his last years). The Stockholm Philharmonic Orchestra plays pieces of music which are associated with the prize winners' home countries.

Professor Fukui shows the solid gold medal that he has just received from the hand of the king. In addition he has also received the diploma. And the money? No, not just yet. The following day he will be present at the offices of the Nobel Foundation where he will receive a check. With the check in his wallet he will be escorted to a bank and what he then does with the money . . . is entirely his own affair.

Aside from the prize money and a gold medal, every Nobel Prize winner receives a personal diploma designed and painted by wellknown Swedish artists. This diploma says that the Royal Swedish Academy of Sciences has awarded Kenichi Fukui and Roald Hoffman the Nobel Prize for their independently developed theories on chemical reaction processes. It is signed by the permanent secretary Tord Ganelius and the President Alf Johnels.

Kungliga
Svenska Vetenskapsakademien
har den 19 oktober 1981 beslutat att med det

NOBELPRIS

som detta år tillerkännes den
som gjort den viktigaste
kemiska upptäckten eller förbättringen
gemensamt belöna

Kenichi Fukui

och Roald Hoffmann
för deras var för sig
utvecklade teorier för kemiska
reaktioners förlopp.

STOCKHOLM DEN 10 DECEMBER 1981

After the ceremonies in the Concert Hall, which take about one hour, a large banquet takes place at the Stockholm Town Hall. The Nobel Banquet has been held here since 1930 and only a fraction of those who would like to take part can be seated. In the main banquet hall there is only enough room for 1 310 dinner guests and no more.

Professor Fukui and his wife Tomoe Fukui arrive at the Nobel Banquet. As they arrive, all the guests pass a huge gathering of press photographers who use this opportunity to take as many pictures as possible as photography is extremely restricted during the actual dinner. At this point the prize winners find that they are no longer alone in the limelight – instead it is their family members who receive all the attention.

Before the banquet can begin, King Karl Gustav and Queen Silvia take the opportunity to get acquainted with the prize winners and their families. The following evening, on December 11th, they will meet again. This time in the Royal Palace in Stockholm where the King and Queen invite all the prize winners home to dinner. The ceremonial procession into the main banquet hall, the Blue Hall. Most of the prize winners com-

ment on the name as the colour blue is nowhere to be seen! When the hall was built in 1923 it was intended that the walls should be covered in blue stucco but everyone thought that the brick walls and the arches were so beautiful that they were left in their natural state. To the sound of ceremonial music from the orchestra, Professor Fukui leads his lady at the table, Princess Lilian, down the majestic staircase. In front of them,

Mrs. Fukui has just descended together with the King, Karl XVI Gustav. All the prize winners and their wives have been placed with a member of the royal family, a member of the government, or a leading dignitary. In order to serve all the 1,300 guests, a staff of 120 waitresses and waiters are required. The Nobel Banquet is such a popular occasion that service people from the entire country line up to get the opportunity to serve at the banquet. Of the 1,300 seats, only 850 are allocated to representatives of the Nobel Foundation. The rest are made available to the Students' Union of Stockholm University, who have their own invitation list and even their own menu. Having acquired a ticket for the banquet and hired a dinner suit or evening dress, the students are given an opportunity to take part "on the sidelines". (The students' tables are arranged along the walls.)

Every year, Swedish television records a program called "Snillen Speku lerar" –Science and Man –in which the Nobel Prize winners are invited to join in an informal discussion on the fundamentals of science. The program is extremely popular and is subsequently sold to a great many countries. It is also extremely well prepared by Bengt Feldreich, the program presenter (right).

A shot from the TV program "Snillen Spekulerar" – Science and Man –in which all the Nobel Prize winners in the fields of Medicine, Chemistry and Physics take part. This impromptu discussion, covers a wide range of scientific subjects, but two specific questions are repeated each year: is there any such thing as scientific intuition, and in what field of research will the Nobel Prizes be given in the year 2000.

At the annual Nobel dinner at the Institute of Technology in Stockholm, the Nobel Prize winners for physics and chemistry are invited to participate, and discussions between the professors and the students are an important part of the enormous flow and exchange of information that takes place during the Nobel week – both within and outside of the official program.

On December 13th the official program of the "Nobel week" is over. Early in the morning the Nobel Prize winners, who all stay at the same hotel, are honored once again in a particularly curious manner. That is the time when Lucia – the queen of light according to Swedish tradition, comes to call. The queen of light and her entourage, are staff from the hotel who pay the prize winners a visit in their rooms in order to signify that light has returned to the darkness of the northern winter. Each year the Nobel Prize winners are equally surprised to see Lucia coming to wake them in the morning. They are told beforehand of what to expect that morning, as the 'queens of light' visit all Swedish homes to wake the citizens with Christmas carols and coffee and buns. But who can really describe what it feels like to be woken up at 6 a.m. by people dressed in white, standing beside your bed singing songs? This, and many other events, are memories for life for the Nobel Prize winners when they return to their homes after their visit to Sweden. For whatever happens in the future, life will never be quite the same again after this very special week in Stockholm when they are given the greatest recognition a scientist can ever receive – the Nobel Prize.

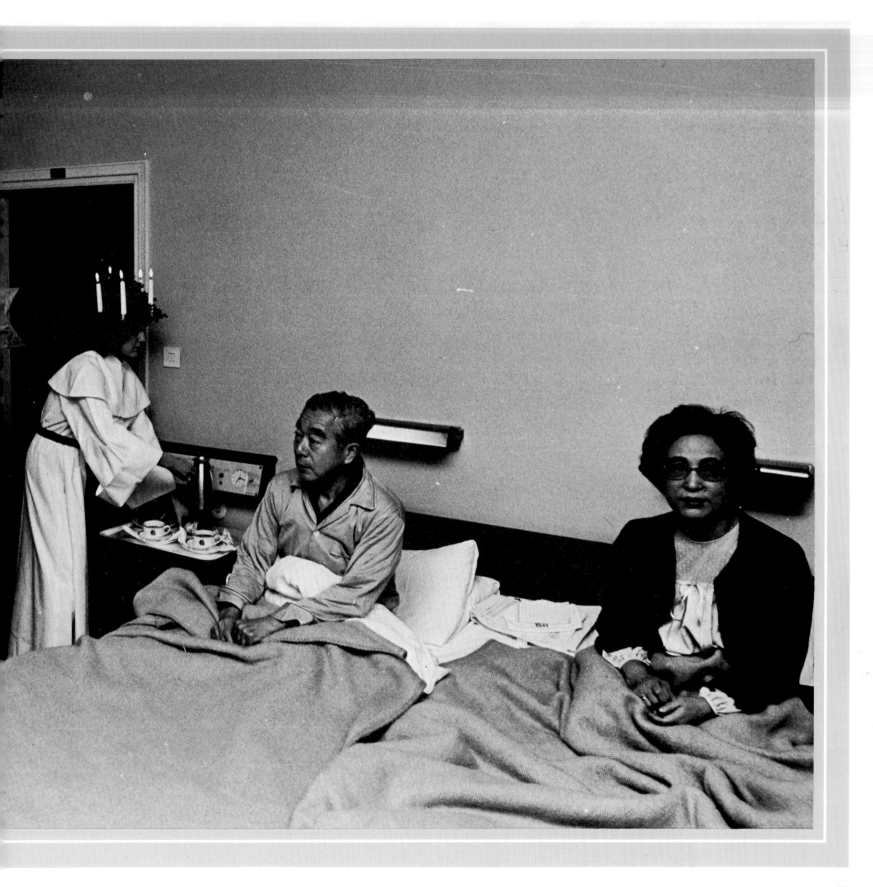

LIFE
AFTER THE
NOBELS

In the spring of 1982 former winners of the Nobel Prize were interviewed. One of the purposes for this book was to provide a focus on the scientific research community whose work is often neglected by an international media which likes to devote its primary attention to the prizewinners in Peace and Literature. Because of the technical nature of their work, scientists remain in a seemingly inaccessable background. Another purpose was to pluck these individuals from their unnecessary obscurity, highlight and present their research and its concerns and thereby create more of a balance among the disciplines.

These interviews probe the existence behind a Nobel prizewinner's public role with questions that sought the small and large realities of their lives in the eye of that storm called the Nobel Prize. What happens to their work and their personal lives after the acceptance speech is made in Stockholm and what do these scientists really think about the Nobel Prize as one of its several hundred recipients?

The following six interviews reflect a range of response on the shape of their lives after receiving the Nobel Prize. Whether they are observing the dark clouds of our galaxy, wondering how the brain generates conscious experience or committed to training individuals from Third World countries for the tasks that will face them upon their return home – each of these six scientists offer an insight into an unknown territory – life after the Nobel Prize.

Dr. Roger W. Sperry, California Institute of Technology, Pasadena, California, USA. Medicine in 1981.

When the Nobel Prize announcement was made on October 9th, 1981, Roger Sperry did not hear about it for several days – he and his wife were camping in a remote part of Baja, California. Remote areas obviously appeal to Dr. Sperry. Indeed, his remarkable entry into what has been called the last frontier – the world of the brain – won the Nobel Prize.

Sperry's research during the 60's unraveled many of the cerebral hemispheres' mysteries and clarified the unique specializations inherent in each. He has been called the extractor of their secrets, revealing that each hemisphere possesses its own conscious world completely independent of the other. These hemispheres are united and informed about each others' activities through a cable of 200 million nerve fibers and yet – as Sperry illuminated in his work with epileptic patients – remote from one another. Separate, conscious worlds.

Sperry has received dozens of honors, degrees and awards throughout his academic and professional life. The list is long and impressive. Winning the Nobel Prize may not be a separate world for a seasoned recipient like Sperry – but it is a *different* world. One suddenly finds oneself at an altitude where the air is thinner, the sun more intense and the view more commanding. Sperry, at 70, reflects on his life post–Nobel one year later:

"I have been lucky and had a medical problem sufficient so that I had an excuse not to make all those speeches, not attend all those banquets or all those interviews and so on, so I have been able to do some work." The Nobel arena is definitely *not* a remote area.

The Nobel Prize clearly generates more instant notoriety for its recipients than all the other prizes combined. "I think it is nice

that people pay more attention to your opinion than before," Sperry admits. The fact is that *more* people pay *more* attention to your opinion an *anything* – from schoe-laces to nuclear energy. Sperry considers himself a lucky man with a medical problem.

In this precipitous arena, Sperry finds it necessary to differentiate between himself as scientist and as private human being. One of the dilemmas winning the Nobel Prize can have is how to answer the interviewers' questions: as the scientist whose brain research was heralded or as the private, philosphical Roger Sperry – when asked a question such as, "What is the most important part of science today?"

Sperry responds, "If I were to be a scientist I would take your question and think about it. And the answer I would come up with might be very different from what I give you off the top of my head." A winner is constantly expected to pivot effortlessly between many roles: the scientist, the private individual and the world citizen.

"The scientist says the whole world is just quantomechanics or particle interaction mechanism. And the humanist says, no, I am more than that and there are other things in the world." Like the hemispheres of the brain, the scientist and the humanist may have different voices but as far as Sperry is concerned, they are not in conflict with one another.

"Our changed view of the relation of mind to brain and the correlated changes in regard to the nature of causality in the relationships of parts to wholes – when these changes are brought in, science comes to stand for something different from what it has stood for and it is no longer in conflict with common sense or humanities or religion," he says. For Sperry, the sciences, the humanities and philosophy all co-exist and when merged, come to stand for something different – an enlarged vision. In Sperry's opinion, the future of the world depends upon their co-existance.

Nobel himself represented this kind of thinking with his selection of medicine, chemistry and physics as the three disciplines which he hoped could provide

answers and solutions for the problems facing his world.

Sperry maintains that these fields are no longer enough and that Nobel, if alive today, would recognize this and respond with choices that bear more directly on the problems of our time. "It is all relevant," says Sperry, "but compared to when it was started I think (their) importance is less, relative to other sciences (and) developments that have occured since."

Interestingly enough, Sperry believes that the absence of population control is the grave problem of our time. "The population problem is interfering with science," he says. "Science is good, it helps the population (which) keeps growing and the problems (get) deeper and deeper. No one knows how to get out of it except to have a nuclear war (or) global famine."

Science can no longer continue to be regarded in conflict with human values but must, as Sperry sees it, begin to inform our values. World governments, in Sperry's view, may be willing to accept "a scientific world view as a kind of compromise."

The over-population problem is "a problem of human values," Sperry maintains. "And that is why I have shifted from my brain problems to human problems because of their key relevance. (Changing)

human values will do it much more humanely than a nuclear war, global famine or some other cataclysmic approach." The philosophical scientist and the scientific philosopher – Sperry embodies this kind of passionate fusion and his career reflects it.

Beginning in 1935, Sperry took an English degree and then a Master's in Psychology at Oberlin College and a Ph. D. in Zoology at the University of Chicago. He became a research fellow in Primate Biology at Harvard and Section Chief in Neuroanatomy at the National Institute of Health. In 1952, he became a Hixon Professor of Psychobiology at CalTech.

Sperry is now thinking and writing about mind-brain relationships and the roles of consciousness and free will which he perceives to have evolved as a directive force in brain function. He is also exploring the ways in which ethical values are intricately involved with subjective experience. Sperry suggests that the domains of ethics and mind-brain are not separate hemispheres at all but rather indelibly inscribed upon one another.

Does he see any breakthroughs in his current research? "It would be nice to find out how the brain generates conscious experience," he muses. "It all comes together in the brain."

Dr. Richard P. Feynman,
California Institute of
Technology, Pasadena,
California, USA.
Physics in 1965.

Dr. Hamilton, O. Smith,
John Hopkins University
Medical School, Baltimore,
Maryland, USA.
Medicine in 1978.

Together, physicist Richard P. Feynman and geneticist Hamilton O. Smith represent an intriguing dichotomy over a rare thing they have in common – both men have won a Nobel Prize. Listening to the two scientists express their views on the legendary Nobel mystique and its power to alter irrevocably the lives of its recipients is like orbiting from the dark to the light side of the moon. Dr. Feynman of the California Institute of Technology was awarded the Physics prize in 1965. Dr. Smith of Johns Hopkins Hospital in Baltimore, Maryland, won the 1978 prize for Physiology/Medicine.

In different conversations, their divergent opinions on the meaning of the Prize raise some interesting questions and dualities.

In his opening remarks, Feynman charges into the bullring with this reflection: "The research I got the Prize for was done in 1947, so by the time I got the prize it had been 18 years during which I continued to research. Even after the Prize, I had some progress in the field. But I had to stop working for a while on account of the Prize." A candid and seldom made statement about the price of public acclaim – that fame can often consume the very work it seeks to honor.

Dr. Smith offers quite another response. Four years after winning the Prize, he states, "I can only answer that all the changes (since the prize) have been good. I am still continuing to do the same sort of research, but in many ways it is much better. I get better students because of the recognition I have achieved, I think funding is a little more easy so that it had an extremely positive effect in almost every way."

Feynman comes forth with what may well be the heart of the paradox: "I think we would be better off without honors – a world without honors! Now with mountains, the difference in height is something we measure very accurately, but human beings in their ability – there is no way to measure." Certainly, an interesting and justifiable belief coming from someone who has actually won a Nobel Prize and a notion antithetical to the tenets of the Nobel tradition, a world composed of the best and the brightest – definitely a world *with* honors.

Speaking with deep personal conviction, Feynman says he thinks the Prize does "... more harm than good. This is a particular personality thing because it depends upon the character of the person what effect the prize and its existance will have on him. I can only refer to my own life – to me it has been a mild annoyance, it bothers me."

Feynman's important reference to character is one that is usually left unexamined in the context of the Nobel Prize. Winning the prize is one thing; the enormous consequences of the Prize are quite another. While one may win the Prize for intellectual achievement, it is one's character which must be prepared and vigilant for the aftermath of the Prize and the demands it makes upon its winners. Feynman realistically suggests that winning the Nobel Prize is not exactly something one can be prepared for.

Back to the visible side of the moon, Dr. Smith concurs enthusiastically with Alfred Nobel's original intentions in creating such a singular award. "If he (Nobel) had in mind giving recognition to certain people who made outstanding contributions in science as a stimulus to young people he has achieved that. It offers more opportunities for researchers there is no question.

Dr Richard P. Feynman

Many people know of you from the recognition of the Prize who would not have heard of you; you are much more, of course, in the public image."

Having a public image suits Dr. Smith infinitely more than it does Dr. Feynman. For Dr. Smith, in the subsequent years since the prize, opportunities have evolved from a recognition he obviously enjoys. "I have certainly many more students who want to work with me, simply because they know about me," he explains. Suddenly they are aware that there is a Dr. Smith who has done an important piece of work and they become aware of what that work is."

In his spare time, Dr. Smith is a consultant for an engineering company. "One is in big demand for that sort of thing. It, of course, looks very good when a company of that sort is asking for public funds and they can say that one of their consultants is a Nobel Prize laureate." One can almost see the knowing smile on Alfred Nobel's face, for he was a scientist who found the time to run his own industry, consolidate trusts and remain in constant search of commercial applications for his laboratory research.

Dr. Smith is nonetheless sensitive to the regard of his peers in this delicate matter of −to win or not to win. "I have colleagues here at the university whom I respect very much. I think they should win a Nobel Prize. Whether they get it or not I am going to respect them quite as much. I would hope to be on the same category even if I had not won the Prize," he muses.

Feynman refers to this kind of potentially dangerous categorization when he says, "I don't think it is fair or right that a guy should have a reputation just because he won a prize. It should be in terms of what he did accomplish and what he is like."

Feynman remembers a party he attended soon after winning the Nobel Prize. "Everything is going fine when suddenly I discover some of them know that I won the Prize and then I am peculiar. I don't feel the human relationship is the same as it was before."

After hearing that he had won a Nobel Prize, Feynman's immediate reaction was to decline the award−a highly unusual

Dr Hamilton O. Smith

gesture, about as frequent as the appearance of Hailey's comet, though not without precedent. Jean-Paul Sartre turned down the Literature Prize in 1964 and Le Duc Tho declined the 1973 Peace Prize which was shared with Henry Kissinger, who accepted. In a second response, Feynman says he "realized that I would make much more trouble for myself and for everybody if I said I was not going to come over and take it. I felt forced, so to speak."

The Nobel Prize is not an end in itself. Life existed before and life certainly goes on afterward. It is an accolade which, according to Feynman, must not be looked upon as an incentive for choosing a career or entering a particular field. He believes

that "the reason to go into science is because nature is interesting, because science is interesting, because your talent is there, because you are inspired by the subject matter, by the character of it, by the people that you meet who are interested in it. That is the reason to do something."

The ideas of Richard Feynman and Hamilton Smith provide an unusual perspective for those of us who live in a world that, for better or for worse, continues to have an revere honors and distinctions of every kind. Even now, the Nobel Institutions are appraising the work of the five individuals who will suddenly find themselves standing forever in a public and perhaps lonely place.

Dr. Ivar Giæver,
General Electric R & D Center, Schenectady, New York, USA.
Physics in 1973.

In age of increasing scientific specialization, Ivar Giaever is a refeshingly curious anomaly. He defines the original meaning of the word *scientist*: One who, through investigation, possesses such knowledge concerned with the physical world and its phenomena. It is an understatement to say that Giaever is innately curious – here is an individual who is fascinated with his environment.

This fascination manifests itself in a variety of fields for Giaever who never stays long in the same place, figuratively speaking. When he immigrated to Canada from his native Norway, he was a mechanical engineer. Once in the United States, he became interested in applied mathematics which eventually led to a degree in physics. His current focus is cellular surfaces which carries him over the threshold and into – biology.

Perhaps it is a fear of stagnation rather than a propensity for boredom which propels Dr. Giaever. He claims he engages with most things because he simply wants to know. "If you change fields, you are forced to rethink and redo things, learn new things, and there are so many new fields to be interested in."

He thinks the Nobel Prize is interesting too – and he happened to win one back in 1973 for the work he was particularly fascinated with in 1960: the tunneling effect of electrons in semiconductors and superconductors. His background knowledge provides well in his present cell study and emphasizes Giaever's unusual spirit of cross-disciplinary contribution.

"As a physicist, I have a lot of advan-

Dr Ivar Giaever sitting on the antique desk which belonged to Thomas A Edison

tages because I understand the extremely complex equipment we use," he says. "Biologists usually don't understand the machinery, but on the other hand, I don't know a great deal about the cells themselves, while biologists know all about them."

Giaever believes that while other prizes may come and go, "the Nobel Prize follows you throughout your lifetime". The instant and lasting fame which the Nobel Prize bestows, have made him aware of the need to become more serious and responsible publically since now, as a bearer of the Prize, he is expected to know infinitely more about infinitely more.

One of Giaever's favorite stories is about Linus Pauling who won the 1954 prize in Chemistry and the 1962 Peace Prize. When asked whether the Prize had changed his life, Dr. Pauling is believed to have said: "No, I was already famous."

This was not true for Dr. Giaever. Forty-four when he won the Prize, he believes that it might be "better to get (the Nobel Prize) when you are older, say when you are 65 or 70–and then become a statesman. Old scientists would make perfect statesmen if they won the Prize!" Unfortunately for Giaever's hypothesis, this is not the case, at least in Physics. The average age of those physicists who have won the Prize in the last decade is approximately 49 years old.

A happy, easygoing man by temperament, Giaever says "getting the Nobel Prize is very complicated. It changes your life. There are more demands on your time and if you continue with science, you are open to much more criticism. You have got to do things you did not do before."

Despite the demands and criticism to which he is exposed, Giaever is generally pleased with the recognition. "It is wonderful and I'm very lucky and happy. But I can be so relaxed because I did not try to get it," he says. "There are people who start out in life so ambitious that everything they do is directed toward winning the Nobel Prize. If you do that, though, you must assemble a team and get the money to support your work. That is perfectly fine because that is how work progresses–if you

have ambitious people who want to do something. But I got the Nobel Prize for work I did by myself. I shared it with Brian Josephson and he always worked alone, too. We didn't have big resources."

One of the finest aspects of the Nobel Prize, according to Giaever, is the public relations work it does for science, which in the aftermath of the Nobel award, leaves its relative obscurity to become front page news. "Winning the Nobel Prize advertises the field," Giaever notes, "People become aware of the fact that there are physicists around, or chemists or doctors."

Giaever is one of thousands of scientists who gravitated to the United States after World War II, attracted by what could be called the exceptional research atmosphere which flourished there. Unlike the smaller

European countries, the U.S. was in a position to spend large amounts of money exclusively on research. And yet a good research atmosphere must have other ingredients besides monetary ones. "I do not think that great progress necessarily comes from money", Giaever maintains. "It comes from people. Naturally, it is true that in certain fields, like high energy physics, you need alot of money to accomplish anything. But this does not apply to all fields."

He continues: "Actually, one reason I like biology is that you don't need a lot of money to do research. All you need is education and the wanting to know." When asked a typical question–what is his research good for–Dr. Giaever is supposed to have responded with nothing but the whole truth: "I do it because I want to know."

Dr. Rosalyn S. Yalow, Bronx Veterans Administration Hospital, Bronx, New York, USA. Medicine in 1977.

Rosalyn Yalow is a New Yorker and the second woman to win a Nobel Prize in Physiology/Medicine. Told she must take stenography courses for a part time secretarial position in order to be admitted into graduate physics courses, Dr. Yalow went on to investigate the application of radioisotopes in blood volume determination and later developed a tool with the potential for measuring circulating insulin in the body. A new era began with this tool, radioimmunoassay which is now used to measure hundreds of biological substances.

Her early interest in mathematics soon transformed into a passion for physics, specifically, nuclear physics. It seemed as if every major experiment brought a Nobel Prize," Dr. Yalow recalls. "Eve Curie had just published the biography of her mother, Marie Curie, which should be a must on the reading list of every young aspiring female scientist. As a Junior at college, I was hanging from the rafters when Enrico Fermi gave a colloquium in January, 1939 on the newly discovered nuclear fission – which has resulted not only in the terror and threat of nuclear warfare but also in the ready availability of radioisotopes for medical investigation and in hosts of other peaceful applications."

In 1941, when Dr. Yalow was offered a physics teaching assistantship at the University of Illinois, she immediately tore up her stenography books. At the first faculty meeting, she discovered herself to be the only woman in the College of Engineering and the first one to be sitting among its 400 members since 1917. She attributes the wartime absence of young men as the reason for her entrance into graduate school. Hardly an excuse, Dr. Yalow offers this as a forthright, historical comment on the conditions under which women were forced to maneuver for jobs and entrance into professional life.

"I would say it is easier today than when I began 40 years ago," Dr. Yalow says frankly about her somewhat solitary quest as a woman scientist. "In other words, legal discrimination, at least in (the United States) has ended. If a woman wants to go into physics nowadays she would not find this type of discrimination. Over the last ten years there has been an enormous increasing opportunity for women to enter medical school. The same thing is happening in other fields. So I would say that nowadays if a woman wants to, she can probably go into any field that she chooses."

After a 40 year career of being "the only woman" in numerous capacities, Dr. Yalow can finally see the beginning of the end of this unnecessarily lonely era. She can look forward to being accompanied by more and more women scientists.

Together with her physicist husband Aaron and moderate household help, Dr. Yalow says they raised two children and "managed to keep the house going". One wonders what layers of truth lie behind such a simple statement – because for women, the matter of career and home life remains a complex one. Dr. Yalow may be

the first Nobel prizewinner to mention the running of a household and the raising of children.

Dr. Yalow had a close affinity with her colleague Dr. Solomon Berson, with whom she formed a 22 year partnership. This invaluable collaboration is always refered to when Yalow speaks of her work and it is clearly her deep regret that Berson did not live to share the Nobel Prize with her. Rosalyn Yalow is someone who does not forget the individuals and experiences which have profoundly shaped her.

Dr. Yalow sees her role in the laboratory "primarily as a thinker" who approaches her research through her personally honed art of investigation. "I think that if anybody can describe what they are going to be doing for the next three or five years, they are not doing investigation – they are doing development," she explains.

She comments on the trajectory of her research: "We did work for a number of years essentially in radiation chemistry which also related to physics, but most of the work has been the application of radio-isotopes in medicine." She elaborates further on the significance of her working relationship with Dr. Berson: "Neither Sol nor I had the advantage of specialized post-doctoral training in investigation. We learned from and disciplined each other and were probably each other's severest critic. I had the good fortune to learn medicine not in a formal medical school but directly from a master of physiology, anatomy and clinical medicine. This training was essential if I were to use my scientific background in areas in which I had no formal education." Here is a vocabulary which relies heavily on the world *our*.

Commenting on a common practice of the Nobel Institutions to award a prize for past work, Dr. Yalow says: "From what I have heard, Alfred Nobel wanted to support recent discoveries and scientists in the prime of their lives. I would say that very often, particularly in biomedical investigation, this is not so. I did not receive the Prize for radium until 1977, although our first major publication in the field was in 1959." Winning the Nobel Prize has not interfered appreciably with Dr. Yalow's work. If any-

thing, it has only fueled an already intense drive.

"My research has not diminished since receiving the Nobel Prize. If anything, I am working much harder because in addition to my research, I have taken on the responsibility of speaking on a number of issues that I believe are important to our society." Having always maintained a heavy schedule of teaching and training in addition to her research work, the Nobel Prize seems to have demanded only a restructuring of her full schedule. It has also meant that she does relatively little routine laboratory work now and is thus free to concentrate on her "professional children" – those who are learning her research techniques and philosophy.

"I am very actively training people. At the moment I have two Japanese scientists with me, two from Mainland China, and one from Uganda. In my other laboratory I also train residents and even medical and college students. They are much more valuable

than technicians would be, so I run the laboratory with very little in the way of technicians."

But now that I usually have six or seven people in training all the time, my primary function is to go around and talk to them and find out what they have just done, how we can interpret it, and how to plan for it in our next experiments."

Her laboratory is infused with the value and necessity of one to one communication. "I have never aspired to have, nor do I now want, a laboratory or a cadre of investigators-in-training that is more extensive than I can personally interact with and supervise."

Yalow is particularly devoted to training people from Third World countries such as China, India and Africa. "I try to work with them on the kinds of problems they will be able to work on after they go home rather than going into problems that are part of the interest of this laboratory. All foreign people who have trained in my laboratory have returned home", she says proudly.

Many prizewinners are susceptible to the lure of becoming consultants for commercial firms who know that an association with the Nobel Prize means good business. Dr. Yalow makes this matter-of-fact statement: "I have never had any association with a commercial enterprise. It is not that I have any objection to cooperating with a commercial firm, it is simply that I never had an offer until after I was already famous. By that time I was more concerned with their interest in exploiting my name rather than in supporting my research."

Perhaps Dr. Yalow's thoughts on the value of the Nobel Prize also echo its psychological value for the women who will look to her as she looked to Marie Curie. "Science was meant to help people. I think that is the real value of the Nobel Prize – its psychological value is important to people of the world. They appreciate that science is for them, and I think it is well for them to recognize that there is something very special about science."

In her reflections on her life and her life's work, Dr. Rosalyn Yalow is a source of uninterrupted clarity.

Dr. Robert W. Wilson,
Bell Laboratories, Holmdel,
New Jersey, USA.
Physics in 1978.

Robert W. Wilson has been an industry sponsored scientist all his professional life. He joined the technical staff at Bell Labs in 1963, fresh out of Caltech as a Ph. D. Research Fellow and has been there ever since. In 1976, he became head of the Radio Physics Department. Two years later he won the Nobel Prize in Physics together with his colleague Arno Penzias, for their discovery of cosmic microwave background radiation. He was 42 years old.

"I sit here comfortably in the Bell Labs (which) has the policy of supporting people fairly well," says Wilson. No struggle for National Science Foundation grants here. Industry provides very well for research if the researchers are resourceful enough. This experience has shaped Robert Wilson's science.

"We can easily pay for astronomy for a long time," Wilson maintains, "just by being clever about what we do." This sounds like a litany of survival among industrial scientists: to continually find commercial application for their research. And even if he could not have anticipated the enormity of Bell Labs, commercial application was one thing Alfred Nobel understood very well.

Wilson continues, "(Nobel), of course, expected that the money was going to make a big difference to someone's research and in my case that did not happen. Bell Labs provide very well for my research and by the time you share a prize around three ways (he and Penzias shared the Prize with Peter L. Kapitza of the Soviet Union) there is not so much money as to make a big difference to someone's research budget which is probably appropriate."

Whatever Nobel's intentions, industry sponsored scientists may be the shape of things to come for future awards – relatively young individuals backed by unlimited resources and for whom satellites rather than typewriters are the office tool.

Whether they like it or not, Nobel Prize winners are in demand by a demanding public. What happens to his work? What about his life? "Certainly a lot more people are asking me to do things," Wilson responds. "For the first three months after the announcement there was preparation for the ceremony, going back, looking at the old work and getting it talked about and a tremendous amount of mail and a lot of interviews. All of that has settled down although it certainly has not stopped." The Nobel Prize is frequently awarded for scientific work done a decade or longer before. Many winners have commented on the strange phenomenon of returning to the "old work" when one is often, as in Wilson's case, light years away mentally.

Wilson and Penzias began their first radio astronomy experiments in the early 60's. Wilson is extremely aware of those around him. He seems to be, by nature, a team worker and when speaking of work he is involved in, he always uses the collective 'we'. His collaboration with Penzias turned out to be fruitful – one that each man made compromises for in order to continue. Wilson relates this story about their early years at Bell Labs:

"With the creation of Comsat by the U.S. Congress, Bell System satellite efforts and related space research were reduced. In 1965, Arno and I were told that the radio astronomy effort could only be supported at the level of one full-time staff member, even though Art Crawford and Rudi Kompfner strongly supported our astronomical research. Arno and I agreed that having two half-time radio astronomers was a better solution to our problem than having one full-time one, so we started taking on other projects."

Aftermath of the Nobel Prize. "I got a call from the local high school yesterday," says Wilson, "can you come and give a talk." I am sure that would not have happened if I had not won the Prize. So it has the effect of my doing many more sort of public things than I would have done otherwise and probably slowed down the research somewhat – but I keep my research going."

Other Nobel laureates have spoken of the problems with slowed-down or stopped research as one of the inevitable side-effects of winning the Prize. These are perhaps difficult transitions for a scientist who has virtually no experience of an audience, especially an audience that is no less than the world itself. Wilson, however, appears to move quite gracefully through the numerous public pressures and expectations. It is the quiet, determined voice of the good scientist who says, "I keep my research going."

Wilson's family may be the key to what keeps him going – they are certainly behind him in his professional efforts – and not invisibly. He speaks of them often. "Our first son, Phillip, was born during my fourth year at Caltech. He had many trips to the Owens Valley Radio Observatory, the first at the age of two weeks. He and (my wife) Betsy were readily accepted at the observatory."

What, after all, did Nobel intend with his controversial will? Wilson believes, "It is about the most important prize and I think that comes partly from Nobel's will and the way it is set up. That the Nobel Prize recognizes the great discoveries in science and therefore when people learn about science they learn about all the people who won Nobel Prizes. All the milestones in their courses are associated with the Nobel Prize so the association goes both ways. A lot of people do not understand the prize very well. They know it is important but they do not understand that it is for a discovery, not for being a good scientist." Perhaps he is reminding himself that after all the glorious recognition and acknowledgement, he must now resume his life as that precursor to all discovery – "a good scientist". One can certainly try to approach this unique problem of winning the Nobel Prize scientifically.

Is there research after the Nobels? For Wilson, a resounding *yes*. "At Bell Labs with radio astronomy there has (over the years) been a lot of tying between astronomy and satellite communications. And we keep both going by using the technology which has been developing at Bell Labs to apply to both," Wilson comments.

"We can do very interesting astronomy with the technology which has been developed for communication purposes." Currently, Wilson is probing the dark clouds of our galaxy with a radio telescope and has discovered that "a sizeable fraction of the gas in our own galaxy is found in such clouds, and furthermore, (these) are the clouds from which new stars are born."

Learning about the universe and how our galaxy is organized is, according to Wilson, the "basic research" he is now engaged in. With no direct commercial application in sight – yet – Wilson says this research provides "an understanding of where we are." The earthly being speaking cosmically.

And where is Dr. Robert Wilson, native son of Texas, at the moment? Even though the sudden exposure as a result of the award may have taken him by surprise, it is the lasting exposure to which he must adapt. Four years later, he still feels that the Prize "is a very nice way to be recognized".

As a Nobel Prize winner, Wilson can expect to be recognized and lauded for the rest of his life. As an astronomer, he has a particularly good perspective. We can remember Dr. Wilson as the man who said, ". . . you think that the rest of the stars are fixed. Because on a human scale they are pretty much fixed. But some of the brightest stars will have a lifetime of only a few million years."

NOBEL PRIZE STATISTICS

Underneath the number and dates themselves, statistics provide stories. Like the underside of a tapestry, the statistics are the knotted threads and the brilliant mural on the other side is the story they tell. Fascinating stories emerge from the 80 plus years of these Nobel statistics. Just one of the stories they hold, is the history of the 20th century.

For example, almost everyone knows that Marie Curie won the Nobel Prize – but do they know she won it twice, in two different fields, something only two individuals have managed to do. Marie Curie won her first Nobel Prize in Physics in 1903 and the Chemistry Prize eight years later; Linus Pauling won the Chemistry Prize in 1954 and the Peace Price in 1962.

Only three persons have ever declined the award, thus perhaps becoming even more legendary. Jean-Paul Sartre declined the 1964 Literature Prize and Le Duc Tho declined the 1973 Peace Prize. Boris Pasternak also declined the 1958 Literature Prize whether or not his was a freely made choice remains shrouded.

In 1939 Hitler's Reich openly forced three German recipients to decline the Prize. Richard Kuhn and Adolf Butenandt. Also, Gerhard Domack "was caused by the authorities of his country to decline" the 1939 Medicine Prize. Later each man was able to receive the diploma and medal.

The two World Wars made it impossible, among other things, to carry out a thorough nominations procedure. The difficulties which these years presented are merely noted with the word *reserved*.

Albert Einstein won the Nobel Prize, but not until 1921 and not for his Special Theory of Relativity which he had come forth with 16 years earlier. He won the Nobel Prize for "his services to Theoretical Physics", in particular his discovery of the photoelectric effect which proved the Theory of Relativity, giving the Committee the definite substantiation it required for his revolutionary theory.

Sir William Lawrence Bragg won the 1915 Nobel Prize in Physics when he was 25 years old and remains the youngest recipient. Interestingly enough, he shared that prize with his father for their work with X-rays. Peter Leonidovitch Kapitsa who won the 1978 Physics Prize at the age of 84, is the oldest recipient.

Only the Peace Committee may award its Nobel Prize to a group or institution, if it chooses. Some of these groups include Amnesty International, the International Labor Organization, and the International Red Cross which received the Peace Prize on three separate occasions.

Four married couples have each won four separate awards; Marie and Piere Curie shared the 1903 Physics Prize; Frederic Joliot and Irene Joliot-Curie shared the 1935 Prize in Chemistry; Gerty Theresa Cori shared the 1947 Medicine Prize with her husband Carl; Gunnar Myrdal won the 1974 Prize in Economics and Alva Myrdal won the 1982 Peace Prize. The Curie women alone are responsible for 3 Nobel Prizes, Marie Curie for two of them and Irene Joliet-Curie for one. Eighteen other women have won Nobel Prizes out of a total of 498 men.

Since the first prize ceremony in 1901 up through 1982, there have been a total number of 536 Nobel laureates. The numerical breakdown of the six disciplines offers some interesting insights. The greatest number of prizes, 135, have been given in Medicine, with the fewest, 79, awarded in Literature. Chemistry and Peace have 99 and 82 laureates, respectively. There have been 20 prizes awarded in Economics since its inclusion into the Nobel realm beginning in 1969.

List of Nobel Laureates*

(Note: Titles, data and places given below refer to the time of the prize-award.)
* We are indebted to the *Nobel Foundation Directory* for the following statistics and information

PHYSICS

1901 RÖNTGEN, WILHELM CONRAD, Germany, Munich University, * 1845, † 1923: *"in recognition of the extraordinary services he has rendered by the discovery of the remarkable rays subsequently named after him"*.

1902 The prize was awarded jointly to:

LORENTZ, HENDRIK ANTOON, The Netherlands, Leyden University, * 1853, † 1928; and

ZEEMAN, PIETER, the Netherlands, Amsterdam University, * 1865, † 1943: *"in recognition of the extraordinary service they rendered by their researches into the influence of magnetism upon radiation phenomena"*.

1903 The prize was divided, one half being awarded to:

BECQUEREL, ANTOINE HENRI, France, Ecole Polytechnique, Paris, * 1852, † 1908: *"in recognition of the extrordinary services he has rendered by his discovery of spontaneous radioactivity"*;

the other half jointly to:

CURIE, PIERRE, France, Ecole municipale de physique et de chimie industrielles, (Municipal School of Industrial Physics and Chemistry), Paris, * 1859, † 1906; and his wife

CURIE, MARIE, née SKLODOWSKA, France, * 1867 (in Warsaw, Poland), † 1934: *"in recognition of the extraordinary services they have rendered by their joint reseaches on the radiation phenomena discovered by Professor Henri Becquerel"*.

1904 RAYLEIGH, Lord (JOHN WILLIAM STRUTT), Great Britain, Royal Institution of Great Britain, London, * 1842, † 1919: *"for his investigations of the densities of the most important gases and for his discovery of argon in connection with these studies"*.

Wilhelm Conrad Röntgen

1905 VON LENARD, PHILIPP EDUARD ANTON, Germany, Kiel University, * 1862 (in Pressburg, then Hungary), † 1947: *"for his work on cathode rays"*.

1906 THOMSON, Sir JOSEPH JOHN, Great Britain, Cambridge University, * 1856, † 1940: *"in recognition of the great merits of his theoretical and experimental investigations on the conduction of electricity by gases"*.

1907 MICHELSON, ALBERT ABRAHAM, U.S.A., Chicago University, * 1852 (in Strelno, then Germany), † 1931: *"for his optical precision instruments and the spectroscopic and metrological investigations carried out with their aid"*.

1908 LIPPMANN, GABRIEL, France, Sorbonne University, Paris, * 1845 (in Hollerich, Luxembourg), † 1921: *"for his method of reproducing colours photographically based on the phenomenon of interference"*.

1909 The prize was awarded jointly to:

MARCONI, GUGLIELMO, Italy, Marconi Wireless Telegraph Co. Ltd., London, Great Britain, * 1874, † 1937; and

BRAUN, CARL FERDINAND, Germany, Strasbourg University, Alsace (then Germany), * 1850, † 1918: *"in recognition of their contributions to the development of wireless telegraphy"*.

1910 VAN DER WAALS, JOHANNES DIDERIK, the Netherlands, Amsterdam University, * 1837, † 1923: *"for his work on the equation of state for gases and liquids".*

1911 WIEN, WILHELM, Germany, Würzburg University, * 1864, † 1928: *"for his discoveries regarding the laws governing the radiation of heat".*

1912 DALÉN, NILS GUSTAF, Sweden, Swedish Gas-Accumulator Co., Lidingö-Stockholm, * 1869, † 1937: *"for his invention of automatic regulators for use in conjunction with gas accumulators for illuminating lighthouses and buoys".*

1913 KAMERLINGH-ONNES, HEIKE, the Netherlands, Leyden University, * 1853, † 1926: *"for his investigations on the properties of matter at low temperatures which led, inter alia, to the production of liquid helium".*

1914 VON LAUE, MAX, Germany, Frankfurt-on-the-Main University, * 1879, † 1960: *for his discovery of the diffraction of X-rays by crystals".*

1915 The prize was awarded jointly to:

BRAGG, Sir WILLIAM HENRY, Great Britain, London University, * 1862, † 1942; and his son

BRAGG, Sir WILLIAM LAWRENCE, Great Britain, Victoria University, Manchester, * 1890 (in Adelaide, Australia), † 1971: *"for their services in the analysis of crystal structure by means of X-rays".*

1916 Reserved.

1917 The prize money for 1916 was allocated to the Special Fund of this prize section.

The prize for 1917: Reserved.

1918 The prize for 1917:

BARKLA, CHARLES GLOVER, Great Britain, Edinburgh University, * 1877, † 1944: *"for his discovery of the characteristic Röntgen radiation of the elements".*

The prize for 1918: Reserved.

1919 The prize for 1918:

PLANCK, MAX KARL ERNST LUDWIG, Germany, Berlin University, * 1858, † 1947: *"in recognition of the services he rendered to the advancement of Physics by his discovery of energy quanta".*

The prize for 1919:

STARK, JOHANNES, Germany, Greifswald University, * 1874, † 1957: *"for his discovery of the Doppler effect in canal rays and the splitting of spectral lines in electric fields."*

1920 GUILLAUME, CHARLES EDOUARD, Switzerland, Bureau International des Poids et Mesures (International Bureau of Weights and Measures), Sèvres, * 1861, † 1938: *"in recognition of the service he has rendered to precision measurements in Physics by his discovery of anomalies in nickel steel alloys".*

1921 Reserved.

1922 The prize for 1921:

EINSTEIN, ALBERT, Germany, Kaiser-Wilhelm-Institut (now Max-Planck-Institut) für Physik, Berlin, * 1879, † 1955: *"for his services to Theoretical Physics, and especially for his discovery of the law of the photoelectric effect".*

The prize for 1922:

BOHR, NIELS, Denmark, Copenhagen University, * 1885, † 1962: *"for his services in the investigation of the structure of atoms and of the radiation emanating from them".*

1923 MILLIKAN, ROBERT ANDREWS, U.S.A., California Institute of Technology, Pasadena, Calif., * 1868, † 1953: *"for his work on the elementary charge of electricity and on the photoelectric effect".*

1924 Reserved.

1925 The prize for 1924:

SIEGBAHN, KARL MANNE GEORG, Sweden, Uppsala University, * 1886, † 1978: *"for his discoveries and research in the field of X-ray spectroscopy".*

The prize for 1925: Reserved.

1926 The prize for 1925 was awarded jointly to:

FRANCK, JAMES, Germany, Goettingen University, * 1882, † 1964; and

HERTZ, GUSTAV, Germany, Halle University, * 1887, † 1975: *"for their discovery of the laws governing the impact of an electron upon an atom".*

The prize for 1926:

PERRIN, JEAN BAPTISTE, France, Sorbonne University, Paris, * 1870, † 1942: *"for his work on the discontinous structure of matter, and especially for his discovery of sedimentation equilibrium".*

1927 The prize was divided equally between:

COMPTON, ARTHUR HOLLY, U.S.A., Chicago University, * 1892, † 1962: *"for his discovery of the effect named after him";* and

WILSON, CHARLES THOMSON REES, Great Britain, Cambridge University, * 1869 (in Glencorse, Scotland), † 1959: *"for his method of making the paths of electrically charged particles visible by condensation of vapour".*

Arthur Holly Compton

1928: Reserved.

1929 The prize for 1928:

RICHARDSON, Sir OWEN WILLANS, Great Britain, London University, * 1879, † 1959: *"for his work on the thermionic phenomenon and especially for the discovery of the law named after him".*

The prize for 1929:

DE BROGLIE, Prince LOUIS-VICTOR, France, Sorbonne University, Institut Henri Poincaré, Paris, * 1892: *"for his discovery of the wave nature of electrons".*

1930 RAMAN, Sir CHANDRASEKHARA VENKATA, India, Calcutta University, * 1888, † 1970: *"for his work on the scattering of light and for the discovery of the effect named after him".*

1931 Reserved.

1932 The prize money for 1931 was allocated to the Special Fund of this prize section.

The prize for 1932: Reserved.

1933 The prize for 1932:

HEISENBERG, WERNER, Germany, Leipzig University, * 1901, † 1976: *"for the creation of quantum mechanics, the application of which has, inter alia, led to the discovery of the allotropic forms of hydrogen".*

The prize for 1933 was awarded jointly to:

SCHRÖDINGER, ERWIN, Austria, Berlin University, Germany, * 1887, † 1961; and

DIRAC, PAUL ADRIEN MAURICE, Great Britain, Cambridge University, * 1902: *"for the discovery of new productive forms of atomic theory".*

1934 Reserved.

1935 The prize money for 1934 was with 1/3 allocated to the Main Fund and with 2/3 to the Special Fund of this prize section.

The prize for 1935:

CHADWICK, Sir JAMES, Great Britain, Liverpool University, * 1891, † 1974: *"for his discovery of the neutron".*

1936 The prize was divided equally between:
HESS, VICTOR FRANZ, Austria, Innsbruck University, * 1883, † 1964: *"for his discovery of cosmic radiation";* and

ANDERSON, CARL DAVID, U.S.A., California Institute of Technology, Pasadena, Calif., * 1905: *"for his discovery of the positron".*

1937 The prize was awarded jointly to:

DAVIDSSON, CLINTON JOSEPH, U.S.A.,

Bell Telephone Laboratories, New York, N.Y., * 1881, † 1958; and

THOMSON, Sir GEORGE PAGET, Great Britain, London University, * 1892, † 1975: *"for their experimental discovery of the diffraction of electrons by crystals".*

1938 FERMI, ENRICO, Italy, Rome University, * 1901, † 1954: *"for his demonstrations of the existence of new radioactive elements produced by neutron irradiation, and for his related discovery of nuclear reactions brought about by slow neutrons".*

Percy Williams Bridgman

1939 LAWRENCE, ERNEST ORLANDO, U.S.A., University of California, Berkeley, Calif., * 1901, † 1958: *"for the invention and development of the cyclotron and for results obtained with it, especially with regard to artificial radioactive elements".*

1940 The prize money was with 1/3 allocated to
–1942 the Main Fund and with 2/3 to the Special Fund of this prize section.

1943 Reserved.

1944 The prize for 1943:

STERN, OTTO, U.S.A., Carnegie Institute of Technology, Pittsburg, Pa., * 1888 (in Sorau, then Germany), † 1969: *"for his contribution to the development of the molecular ray method and his discovery of the magnetic moment of the proton".*

The prize for 1944:

RABI, ISIDOR ISAAC, U.S.A., Columbia University, New York, N.Y., * 1898 (in Rymanow, then Austria-Hungary): *"for his resonance method for recording the magnetic properties of atomic nuclei".*

1945 PAULI, WOLFGANG, Austria, Princeton University, N.J., U.S.A., * 1900 (in Vienna), † 1958: *"for the discovery of the Exclusion Principle, also called the Pauli Principle".*

1946 BRIDGMAN, PERCY WILLIAMS, U.S.A., Harvard University, Cambridge, Mass., * 1882, † 1961: *"for the invention of an apparatus to produce extremely high pressures, and for the discoveries he made therewith in the field of high pressure physics".*

1947 APPLETON, Sir EDWARD VICTOR, Great Britain, Department of Scientific and Industrial Research, London, * 1892, † 1965: *"for his investigations of the physics of the upper atmosphere especially for the discovery of the so-called Appleton layer".*

1948 BLACKETT, Lord PATRICK MAYNARD STUART, Great Britain, Victoria University, Manchester, * 1897, † 1974: *"for his development of the Wilson cloud chamber method, and his discoveries therewith in the fields of nuclear physics and cosmic radiation".*

1949 YUKAWA, HIDEKI, Japan, Kyoto Imperial University, Visiting Professor Columbia University, New York, N.Y., U.S.A., * 1907 † 1981: *"for his prediction of the existence of measons on the basis of theoretical work on nuclear forces".*

1950 POWELL, CECIL FRANK, Great Britain, Bristol University, * 1903, † 1969: *"for his development of the photographic method of studying nuclear processes and his discoveries regarding mesons made with this method".*

1951 The prize was awarded jointly to:

COCKCROFT, Sir JOHN DOUGLAS, Great Britain, Atomic Energy Research Establishment, Harwell, Didcot, Berks., * 1897, † 1967; and

WALTON, ERNEST THOMAS SINTON, Ireland, Dublin University, * 1903: *"for their pioneer work on the transmutation of atomic nuclei by artificially accelerated atomic particles".*

1952 The prize was awarded jointly to:

BLOCH, FELIX, U.S.A., Stanford University, Stanford, Calif., * 1905 (in Zurich, Switzerland); and

PURCELL, EDWARD MILLS, U.S.A., Harvard University, Cambridge, Mass., * 1912: *"for their development of new methods for nuclear magnetic precision measurements and discoveries in connection therewith".*

1953 ZERNIKE; FRITS (FREDERIK), the Netherlands, Groningen University, * 1888, † 1966: *"for his demonstraion of the phase contrast method, especially for his invention of the phase contrast microscope".*

1954 The prize was divided equally between:

BORN, MAX, Great Britain, Edinburgh University, * 1882 (in Breslau, then Germany), † 1970: *"for his fundamental research in quantum mechanics, especially for his statistical interpretation of the wave-function",* and

BOTHE; WALTHER, Germany, Heidelberg University, Max-Planck-Institut (former Kaiser-Wilhelm-Institut) für medizinische Forschung, Heidelberg, * 1891, † 1957: *"for the coincidence method and his discoveries made therewith".*

1955 The prize was divided equally between

LAMB, WILLIS EUGENE, U.S.A. Stanford University, Stanford, Calif., * 1913: *"for his discoveries concerning the fine structure of the hydrogen spectrum";* and

KUSCH, POLYKARP, U.S.A., Columbia University, New York, N.Y., * 1911 (in Blankenburg, then Germany): *"for his precision determination of the magnetic moment of the electron".*

1956 The prize was awarded jointly, one third each, to:

SHOCKLEY, WILLIAM, U.S.A., Semiconductor Laboratory of Beckman Instruments, Inc., Mountain View, Calif., * 1910 (in London, Great Britain);

BARDEEN, JOHN, U.S.A., University of Illinois, Urbana, Ill., * 1908; and

BRATTAIN, WALTER HOUSER, U.S.A., Bell Telephone Laboratories, Murray Hill, N.J., * 1902: *"for their researches on semiconductors and their discovery of the transistor effect".*

1957 The prize was awarded jointly to:

YANG, CHEN NING, China, Institute for Advanced Study, Princeton, N.J., U.S.A., * 1922; and

LEE, TSUNG-DAO, China, Columbia University, New York, U.S.A., * 1926: *"for their penetrating investigation of the so-called parity laws which has led to important discoveries regarding the elementary particles".*

1958 The prize was awarded jointly to:

ČERENKOV, PAVEL ALEKSEJVIČ, USSR, Physics Institute of USSR Academy of Sciences, Moscow, * 1904;

FRANK, ILJA MICHAJLOVIČ, USSR, University of Moscow and Physics Institute of USSR Academy of Sciences, Moscow, * 1908; and

TAMM, IGOR JEVGENÉVIČ, USSR, University of Moscow and Physics Institute of USSR Academy of Sciences, Moscow, * 1895, † 1971: *"for the discovery and the interpretation of the Cerenkov effect".*

1959 The prize was awarded jointly to;

SEGRÈ, EMILIO GINO, U.S.A., University of California, Berkeley, Calif., * 1905 (in Tivoli, Italy); and

CHAMBERLAIN, OWEN, U.S.A., University of California, Berkeley, Calif., * 1920: *"for their discovery of the antiproton".*

1960 GLASER, DONALD, A., U.S.A., University of California, Berkeley, Calif., * 1926: *"for the invention of the bubble chamber".*

1961 The prize was divided equally between:

HOFSTADTER, ROBERT, U.S.A., Stanford University, Stanford, Calif., * 1915: *"for his pioneering studies of electron scattering in atomic nuclei and for his thereby achieved discoveries concerning the structure of the nucleons";* and

MÖSSBAUER, RUDOLF LUDWIG, Germany, Technische Hochschule, Munich, at present California Institute of Technology, Pasadena, California, U.S.A., * 1929: *"for his researches concerning the resonance ab-*

sorption of gamma radiation and his discovery in this connection of the effect which bears his name".

1962 LANDAU, LEV DAVIDOVIČ, USSR, Academy of Sciences, Moscow, * 1908, † 1968: *"for his pioneering theories for condensed matter, especially liquid helium".*

Owen Chamberlain

1963 The prize was divided, one half being awarded to:

WIGNER, EUGENE, P., U.S.A., Princeton University, Princeton, N.J., * 1902 (in Budapest): *"for his contributions to the theory of the atomic nucleus and the elementary particles, particularly through the discovery and application of fundamental symmetry principles";* and the other half jointly to:

GOEPPERT-MAYER, MARIA, U.S.A., University of California, La Jolla, Calif., * 1906 (in Kattowitz, then Germany), † 1972; and

JENSEN, J. HANS D., Germany, University of Heidelberg, * 1907, † 1973: *"for their discoveries concerning nuclear shell structure".*

1964 The prize was divided, one half being awarded to:

TOWNES, CHARLES HARD, U.S.A., Massachusetts Institute of Technology, Cambridge, Mass., * 1915; and the other half jointly to:

BASOV, NIKOLAI GENNADIEVIČ, USSR, Lebedev Institute for Physics, Akademija Nauk, Moscow, * 1922; and

PROCHOROV, ALEKSANDRE MIKHAILOVIČ, USSR, Lebedev Institute for Physics, Akademija Nauk, Moscow, * 1916: *"for fundamental work in the field of quantum electronics, which has led to the construction of oscillators and amplifiers based on the maser-laser-principle".*

1965 The prize was awarded jointly to:

TOMONAGA, SIN-ITIRO, Japan, Tokyo, University of Education, Tokyo, * 1906, † 1979;

SCHWINGER, JULIAN, U.S.A., Harvard University, Cambridge, Mass., * 1918; and

FEYNMAN, RICHARD, P., U.S.A., California Institute of Technology, Pasadena, Calif., * 1918: *"for their fundamental work in quantum electrodynamics, with deep-ploughing consequences for the physics of elementary particles".*

1966 KASTLER, ALFRED, France, École Normale Supérieure, Université de Paris, Paris, * 1902: *"for the discovery and development of optical methods for studying hertzian resonances in atoms".*

1967 BETHE, HANS ALBRECHT, U.S.A., Cornell University, Ithaca, N.Y., * 1906 (in Strasbourg, then Germany): *"for his contributions to the theory of nuclear reactions, especially his discoveries concerning the energy production in stars".*

1968 ALVAREZ, LUIS, W., U.S.A., University of California, Berkeley, Calif., * 1911: *"for his decisive contributions to elementary particle physics, in particular the discovery of a large number of resonance states, made possible through his development of the technique of using hydrogen bubble chamber and data analysis".*

1969 GELL-MANN, MURRAY, U.S.A., California Institute of Technology, Pasadena, California, * 1929: *"for his contributions and discoveries concerning the classification of elementary particles and their interactions".*

1970 The prize was divided equally between:

ALFVÉN, HANNES, Sweden, Royal Institute of Technology, Stockholm, * 1908: *"for fundamental work and discoveries in magneto-hydrodynamics with fruitful applications in different parts of plasma physics";* and

NÉEL, LOUIS, France, University of Grenoble, Grenoble, * 1904: *"for fundamental work and discoveries concerning antiferromagnetism and ferrimagnetism which have led to important applications in solid state physics".*

Hannes Alfvén

1971 GABOR, DENNIS, Great Britain, Imperial College of Science and Technology, London, * 1900 (in Budapest, Hungary), † 1979: *"for his invention and development of the holographic method".*

1972 The prize was awarded jointly to:

BARDEEN, JOHN, U.S.A., University of Illinois, Urbana, * 1908;

COOPER, LEON, N., U.S.A., Brown University, Providence, Rhode Island, * 1930, and

SCHRIEFFER, J, ROBERT, U.S.A., University of Pennsylvania, Philadelphia, * 1931: *"for their jointly developed theory of superconductivity, usually called the BCS-theory".*

1973 The prize was divided, one half being equally shared between:

ESAKI, LEO, Japan, IBM Thomas J. Watson Research Center, Yorktown Heights, N.Y., U.S.A., * 1925, and

GIAEVER, IVAR, U.S.A., General Electric Company, Schenectady, N.Y., * 1929 (in Bergen, Norway): *"for their experimental discoveries regarding tunneling phenomena in semiconductors and superconductors, respectively",*

and the other half awarded to:

JOSEPHSON, BRIAN, D., Great Britain, Cambridge University, Cambridge, * 1940: *"for his theoretical predictions of the properties of a supercurrent through a tunnel barrier, in particular those phenomena which are generally known as the Josephson effects".*

1974 The prize was awarded jointly to:

RYLE, Sir MARTIN, Great Britain, University of Cambridge, Cambridge, * 1918; and

HEWISH, ANTONY, Great Britain, University of Cambridge, Cambridge, * 1924: *"for their pioneering research in radio astrophysics: Ryle for his observations and inventions, in particular of the aperture synthesis technique, and Hewish for his decisive role in the discovery of pulsars".*

1975 The prize was awarded to:

BOHR, AAGE, Denmark, Niels Bohr Institute, Copenhagen, * 1922;

MOTTELSON, BEN, Denmark, Nordita, Copenhagen, * 1926 (in Chicago, U.S.A.), and

RAINWATER, JAMES, U.S.A., Columbia University, New York, * 1917: *"for the discovery of the connection between collective motion and particle motion in atomic nuclei and the development of the theory of the structure of the atomic nucleus based on this connection".*

1976 The prize was divided equally between:

RICHTER, BURTON, U.S.A., Stanford Linear Accelerator Center, Stanford, California, * 1931;

TING, SAMUEL C.C., U.S.A., Massachusetts Institute of Technology, Cambridge (European Center for Nuclear Research, Geneva, Switzerland), * 1936: *"for their pioneering work in the discovery of a heavy elementary particle of a new kind".*

1977 The prize was divided equally between:

ANDERSON, PHILIP W., U.S.A., Bell Laboratories, Murray Hill, New Jersey, * 1923;

MOTT, Sir NEVILL, F., Great Britain, Cambridge University, Cambridge, * 1905 and

VAN VLECK, JOHN H., U.S.A., Harvard University, Cambridge, Mass., * 1899, † 1980: *"for their fundamental theoretical investigations of the electronic structure of magnetic and disordered systems".*

1978 The prize was divided, one half being awarded to:

KAPITSA, PETER LEONIDOVITCH, USSR, Academy of Sciences, Moscow, * 1894: *"for his basic inventions and discoveries in the area of low-temperature physics",*

and the other half divided equally between:

PENZIAS, ARNO A., U.S.A., Bell Laboratories, Holmdel, New Jersey, * 1933 (in Munich, Germany) and

WILSON, ROBERT W., U.S.A., Bell Laboratories, Holmdel, New Jersey, * 1936: *"for their discovery of cosmic microwave background radiation".*

1979 The prize was divided equally between:

GLASHOW, SHELDON L., U.S.A., Lyman Laboratory, Harvard University, Cambridge, * 1932;

SALAM, ABDUS, Pakistan, International Centre for Theoretical Physics, Trieste, and Imperial College of Science and Technology, London, England, * 1926 and

WEINBERG, STEVEN, U.S.A., Harvard University, Cambridge, * 1933: *"for their contributions to the theory of the unified weak and electromagnetic interaction between elementary particles, including inter alia the prediction of the weak neutral current".*

Jacobus Henricus Van't Hoff

1980 The prize was divided equally between:

CRONIN, JAMES W., U.S.A., University of Chicago, Chicago Ill., * 1931 and

FITCH, VAL L., U.S.A., Princeton University, Princeton, New Jersey, * 1923: *"for the discovery of violations of fundamental symmetry principles in the decay of neutral K-mesons".*

1981 The prize was awarded by one half jointly to:

BLOEMBERGEN, NICOLAAS, U.S.A., Harvard University, Cambridge, Mass., U.S.A., * 1920 and

SCHAWLOW, ARTHUR L., U.S.A., Stanford University, Stanford, Cal., U.S.A., * 1921: *"for their contribution to the development of laser spectroscopy".*

and the other half to:

SIEGBAHN, KAI M., Sweden, Uppsala University, Uppsala, Sweden, * 1918: *"for his contribution to the development of high-resolution electron spectroscopy".*

1982 WILSON, KENNETH G., U.S.A., Cornell University, Ithaca, N.Y., U.S.A., * 1936: *"for his theory for critical phenomena in connection with phase transitions".*

1901 VAŃT HOFF, JACOBUS HENRICUS, the Netherlands, Berlin University, Germany, * 1852, † 1911: *"in recognition of the extraordinary services he has rendered by the discovery of the laws of chemical dynamics and osmotic pressure in solutions".*

1902 FISCHER, HERMANN EMIL, Germany, Berlin University, * 1852, † 1919: *"in recognition of the extraordinary services he has rendered by his work on sugar and purine syntheses".*

1903 ARRHENIUS, SVANTE AUGUST, Sweden, Stockholm University, * 1859, † 1927: *"in recognition of the extraordinary services he has rendered to the advancement of chemistry by his electrolytic theory of dissociation".*

1904 RAMSAY, Sir WILLIAM, Great Britain, London University, * 1852, † 1916: *"in recognition of his services in the discovery of the inert gaseous elements in air, and his determination of their place in the periodic system".*

1905 VON BAEYER, JOHANN FRIEDRICH WILHELM ADOLF, Germany, Munich University, * 1835, † 1917: *"in recognition of his services in the advancement of organic chemistry and the chemical industry, through his work on organic dyes and hydroaromatic compounds".*

1906 MOISSAN, HENRI, France, Sorbonne University, Paris, * 1852, † 1907: *"in recognition of the great services rendered by him in his investigation and isolation of the element fluorine, and for the adoption in the service of science of the electric furnace called after him".*

1907 BUCHNER, EDUARD, Germany, Landwirtschaftliche Hochschule (Agricultural College), Berlin, * 1860, † 1917: *"for his biochemical researches and his discovery of cellfree fermentation".*

1908 RUTHERFORD, Lord ERNEST, Great Britain, Victoria University, Manchester, * 1871 (in Nelson, New Zealand), † 1937: *"for his investigations into the disintegration of the elements, and the chemistry of radioactive substances".*

1909 OSTWALD, WILHELM, Germany, Leipzig University, * 1853 (in Riga, then Russia), † 1932: *"in recognition of his work on catalysis and for his investigations into the fundamental principles governing chemical equilibria and rates of reaction".*

1910 WALLACH, OTTO, Germany, Goettingen University, * 1847, † 1931: *"in recognition of his services to organic chemistry and the chemical industry by his pioneer work in the field of alicyclic compounds".*

1911 CURIE, MARIE, née SKLODOWSKA, France, Sorbonne University, Paris, * 1867 (in Warsaw, Poland), † 1934: *"in recognition of her services to the advancement of chemistry by the discovery of the elements radium and polonium, by the isolation of radium and the study of the nature and compounds of this remarkable element".*

Marie Curie

1912 The prize was divided equally between:

GRIGNARD, VICTOR, France, Nancy University, * 1871, † 1935: *"for the discovery of the so-called Grignard reagent, which in recent years has greatly advanced the progress of organic chemistry";* and

SABATIER, PAUL, France, Toulouse University, * 1854, † 1941: *"for his method of hydrogenating organic compounds in the pre-*sence of finely disintegrated metals whereby the progress of organic chemistry has been greatly advanced in recent years".*

1913 WERNER, ALFRED, Switzerland, Zurich University, * 1866 (in Mulhouse, Alsace, then Germany), † 1919: *"in recognition of his work on the linkage of atoms in molecules by which he has thrown new light on earlier investigations and opened up new fields of research especially in inorganic chemistry"*

1914 Reserved.

1915 The prize for 1914:

RICHARDS, THEODORE WILLIAM, U.S.A., Harvard University, Cambridge, Mass., * 1868, † 1928: *"in recognition of his accurate determinations of the atomic weight of a large number of chemical elements".*

The prize for 1915:

WILLSTÄTTER, RICHARD MARTIN, Germany, Munich University, * 1872, † 1942: *"for his researches on plant pigments, especially chlorophyll".*

1916 Reserved.

1917 The prize money for 1916 was allocated to the Special Fund of this prize section.

The prize for 1917: Reserved.

1918 The prize money for 1917 was allocated to the Special Fund of this prize section.

The prize for 1918: Reserved.

1919 The prize for 1918:

HABER, FRITZ, Germany, Kaiser-Wilhelm-Institut (now Fritz-Haber-Institut) für physikalische Chemie und Electrochemie, Berlin-Dahlem, * 1868, † 1934: *"for the synthesis of ammonia from its elements".*

The prize for 1919: Reserved.

1920 The prize money for 1919 was allocated to the Special Fund of this prize section.

The prize for 1920: Reserved.

1921 The prize for 1920:

NERNST, WALTHER HERMANN, Germany, Berlin University, * 1864, † 1941: *in recognition of his work in thermochemistry".*

The prize for 1921: Reserved.

1922 The prize for 1921:

SODDY, FREDERICK, Great Britain, Oxford University, * 1877, † 1956: *"for his contributions to our knowledge of the chemistry of radioactive substances, and his investigations into the origin and nature of isotopes".*

The prize for 1922:

ASTON, FRANCIS WILLIAM, Great Britain, Cambridge University, * 1877, † 1945: *"for his discovery, by means of his mass spectrograph, of isotopes in a large number of non-radioactive elements, and for his enunciation of the whole-number rule".*

1923 PREGL, FRITZ, Austria, Graz University, * 1869, † 1930: *"for his invention of the method of micro-analysis of organic substances".*

1924 Reserved.

1925 The prize money for 1924 was allocated to the Special Fund of this prize section.

The prize for 1925: Reserved.

1926 The prize for 1925:

ZSIGMONDY, RICHARD ADOLF, Germany, Goettingen University, * 1865 (in Vienna, Austria), † 1929: *"for his demonstration of the heterogenous nature of colloid solutions and for the methods he used, which have since become fundamental in modern colloid chemistry".*

The prize for 1926:

SVEDBERG, THE (THEODOR), Sweden, Uppsala University, * 1884, † 1971: *"for his work on disperse systems".*

1927 Reserved.

1928 The prize for 1927:

WIELAND, HEINRICH OTTO, Germany, Munich University, * 1877, † 1957: *for his investigations of the constitution of the bile acids and related substances".*

The prize for 1928:

WINDAUS, ADOLF OTTO REINHOLD, Germany, Goettingen University, * 1876, † 1959: *"for the services rendered through his research into the constitution of the sterols and their connection with the vitamins".*

1929 The prize was divided equally between:

HARDEN, Sir ARTHUR, Great Britain, London University, *1865, † 1940; and

VON EULER-CHELPIN, HANS KARL AUGUST SIMON, Sweden, Stockholm University, * 1873 (in Augsburg, Germany), † 1964: "for their investigations on the fermentation of sugar and fermentative enzymes".

1930 FISCHER, HANS, Germany, Technische Hochschule (Institute of Technology), Munich, * 1881, † 1945: "for his researches into the constitution of haemin and chlorophyll and especially for his synthesis of haemin".

1931 The prize was awarded jointly to:

BOSCH, CARL, Germany, Heidelberg University and I.G. Farbenindustrie A.G., Heidelberg, * 1874, † 1940; and

BERGIUS, FRIEDRICH, Germany, Heidelberg, and I.G. Farbenindustrie A.G., Mannheim-Rheinau, * 1884, † 1949: "in recognition of their contributions to the invention and development of chemical high pressure methods".

1932 LANGMUIR, IRVING, U.S.A., General Electric Co., Schenectady, N.Y., * 1881, † 1957: "for his discoveries and investigations in surface chemistry".

1933 Reserved.

1934 The prize money for 1933 was with 1/3 allocated to the Main Fund and with 2/3 to the Special Fund of this prize section.

The prize for 1934:

UREY, HAROLD CLAYTON, U.S.A., Columbia University, New York, N.Y., * 1893, † 1981: "for his discovery of heavy hydrogen".

1935 The prize was awarded jointly to:

JOLIOT, FRÉDÉRIC, France, Institut du Radium, Paris, * 1900, † 1958; and his wife

JOLIOT-CURIE, IRÈNE, France, Institut du Radium, Paris, * 1897, † 1956: "in recognition of their synthesis of new radioactive elements".

1936 DEBYE, PETRUS (PETER) JOSEPHUS WILHELMUS, the Netherlands, Berlin University, and Kaiser-Wilhelm-Institut (now Max-Planck-Institut) für Physik, Berlin-Dahlem, Germany, * 1884, † 1966: "for his

contributions to our knowledge of molecular structure through his investigations on dipole moments and on the diffraction of X-rays and electrons in gases".

1937 The prize was divided equally between:

HAWORTH, Sir WALTER NORMAN, Great Britain, Birmingham University, * 1883, † 1950: "for his investigations on carbohydrates and vitamin C"; and

KARRER, PAUL, Switzerland, Zurich University, * 1889, † 1971: "for his investigations on carotenoids, flavins and vitamins A and B²".

1938 Reserved.

1939 The prize for 1938:

KUHN, RICHARD, Germany, Heidelberg University and Kaiser-Wilhelm-Institut (now Max-Planck-Institut) für medizinische Forschung, Heidelberg, * 1900 (in Vienna, Austria), † 1967: "for his work on carotenoids and vitamins. (Caused by the authorities of his country to decline the award but later received the diploma and the medal.)

The prize for 1939 was divided equally between:

BUTENANDT, ADOLF FRIEDRICH JOHANN, Germany, Berlin University and Kaiser-Wilhelm-Institut (now Max-Planck-Institut) für Biochemie, Berlin-Dahlem, * 1903: "for his work on sex hormones". (Caused by the authorities of his country to decline the award but later received the diploma and the medal); and

RUŽIČKA, LEOPOLD, Switzerland, Eidgenössische Technische Hochschule (Federal Institute of Technology), Zurich, * 1887 (in Vukovar, then Austria-Hungary), † 1976: "for his work on polymethylenes and higher terpenes".

1940 The prize money was with 1/3 allocated to
–1942 the Main Fund and with 2/3 to the Special Fund of this prize section.

1943 Reserved.

1944 The prize for 1943:

DE HEVESY, GEORGE, Hungary, Stockholm University, Sweden, * 1885, † 1966: "for his work on the use of isotopes as tracers in the study of chemical processes".

The prize for 1944: Reserved.

Adolf Friedrich Johann Butenandt

1945 The prize for 1944:

HAHN, OTTO, Germany, Kaiser-Wilhelm-Institut (now Max-Planck-Institut) für Chemie, Berlin-Dahlem, * 1879, † 1968: "for his discovery of the fission of heavy nuclei".

The prize for 1945:

VIRTANEN, ARTTURI, ILMARI, Finland, Helsinki University, * 1895, † 1973: "for his research and inventions in agricultural and nutrition chemistry, especially for his fodder preservation method".

1946 The prize was divided, one half being awarded to:

SUMNER, JAMES BATCHELLER, U.S.A., Cornell University, Ithaca, N.Y., * 1887, † 1955: "for his discovery that enzymes can be crystallized".

the other half jointly to:

NORTHROP, JOHN HOWARD, U.S.A., Rockefeller Institute for Medical Reseach, Princeton, N.J., * 1891; and

STANLEY, WENDELL MEREDITH, U.S.A., Rockefeller Institute for Medical Research,

Princeton, N.J., * 1904, † 1971: *"for their preparation of enzymes and virus proteins in a pure form"*.

1947 ROBINSON, Sir ROBERT, Great Britain, Oxford Unviersity, * 1886, † 1975: *"for his investigations on plant products of biological importance, especially the alkaloids"*.

1948 TISELIUS, ARNE WILHELM KAURIN, Sweden, Uppsala University, * 1902, † 1971: *"for his research on electrophoresis and adsorption analysis, especially for his discoveries concerning the complex nature of the serum proteins"*.

1949 GIAUQUE, WILLIAM FRANCIS, U.S.A., University of California, Berkeley, Calif., * 1895 † 1982: *"for his contributions in the field of chemical thermodynamics, particularly concerning the behaviour of substances at extremely low temperatures"*.

1950 The prize was awarded jointly to:

DIELS, OTTO PAUL HERMANN, Germany, Kiel University, * 1876, † 1954; and

ALDER, KURT, Germany, Cologne University, * 1902, † 1958: *"for their discovery and development of the diene synthesis"*.

1951 The prize was awarded jointly to:

McMILLAN, EDWIN MATTISON, U.S.A., University of California, Berkeley, Calif., * 1907; and

SEABORG, GLENN, THEODORE, U.S.A., University of California, Berkeley, Calif., * 1912: *"for their discoveries in the chemistry of the transuranium elements"*.

1952 The prize was awarded jointly to

MARTIN, ARCHER JOHN PORTER, Great Britain, National Institute for Medical Research, London, * 1910; and

SYNGE, RICHARD LAURENCE MILLINGTON, Great Britain, Rowett Research Institute, Bucksburn (Scotland), * 1914: *"for their invention of partition chromatography"*.

1953 STAUDINGER, HERMANN, Germany, University of Freiburg im Breisgau and Staatliches Institut für makromolekulare Chemie (State Reseach Institute for Macromolecular Chemistry), Freiburg in Br., * 1881, † 1965: *"for his discoveries in the field of macromolecular chemistry"*.

1954 PAULING, LINUS CARL, U.S.A., California Institute of Technology, Pasadena, Calif., * 1901: *"for his reseach into the nature of the chemical bond and its application to the elucidation of the structure of complex substances"*.

1955 DU VIGNEAUD, VINCENT, U.S.A., Cornell University, New York, N.Y., * 1901, † 1978: *"for his work on biochemically important sulphur compounds, especially for the first synthesis of a polypeptide hormone"*.

1956 The prize was awarded jointly to:

HINSHELWOOD, Sir CYRIL NORMAN, Great Britain, Oxford University, * 1897, † 1867; and

SEMENOV, NIKOLAJ NIKOLAJEVIČ, USSR, Institute for Chemical Physics of the Academy of Sciences of the USSR, Moscow, * 1896: *"for their researches into the mechanism of chemical reactions"*.

Melvin Calvin

1957 TODD, Lord ALEXANDER R., Great Britain, Cambridge University, * 1907: *"for his work on nucleotides and nucleotide co-enzymes"*.

1958 SANGER, FREDERICK, Great Britain, Cambridge University, * 1918: *"for his work on the structure of proteins, especially that of insulin"*.

1959 HEYROVSKÝ, JAROSLAV, Czechoslovakia, Polarographic Institute of the Czechoslovak Academy of Science, Prague, * 1890, † 1967: *"for his discovery and development of the polarographic methods of analysis"*.

1960 LIBBY, WILLARD FRANK, U.S.A., University of California, Los Angeles, Calif., * 1908, † 1980: *"for his method to use carbon-14 for age determination in archaeology, geology, geophysics, and other branches of science"*.

1961 CALVIN, MELVIN, U.S.A., University of California, Berkeley, California, * 1911: *"for his research on the carbon dioxide assimilation in plants"*.

1962 The prize was divided equally between:

PERUTZ, MAX FERDINAND, Great Britain, Laboratory of Molecular Biology, Cambridge, * 1914 (in Vienna); and

KENDREW, Sir JOHN COWDERY, Great Britain, Laboratory of Molecular Biology, Cambridge, * 1917: *"for their studies of the structures of globular proteins"*.

1963 The prize was divided equally between:

ZIEGLER, KARL, Germany, Max-Planck-Institut für Kohlenforschung (Max-Planck-Institute for Carbon Reseach), Mülheim/Ruhr, * 1898, † 1973; and

NATTA, GIULIO, Italy, Institute of Technology, Milan, * 1903, † 1979: *"for their discoveries in the field of the chemistry and technology of high polymers"*.

1964 HODGKIN, DOROTHY CROWFOOT, Great Britain, Royal Society, Oxford University, Oxford, * 1910: *"for her determinations by X-ray techniques of the structures of important biochemical substances"*.

1965 WOODWARD, ROBERT BURNS, U.S.A., Harvard University, Cambridge, Mass., * 1917, † 1979: *"for his outstanding achievements in the art of organic synthesis"*.

1966 MULLIKEN, ROBERT S., U.S.A., University of Chicago, Ill., * 1896: *"for his fundamental work concerning chemical bonds and the electronic structure of molecules by the molecular orbital method"*.

1967 The prize was divided, one half being awarded to:

EIGEN, MANFRED, Federal Republic of

Germany, Max-Planck-Institut für Physikalische Chemie, Göttingen, * 1927;

and the other half jointly to:

NORRISH, RONALD GEORGE WREYFORD, Great Britain, Institute of Physical Chemistry, Cambridge, * 1897, † 1978; and

PORTER, Sir GEORGE, Great Britain, The Royal Institution, London, * 1920: *"for their studies of extremely fast chemical reactions, effected by disturbing the equilibrium by means of very short pulses of energy".*

1968 ONSAGER, LARS, U.S.A., Yale University, New Haven, Conn., * 1903 (in Oslo, Norway), † 1976: *"for the discovery of the reciprocal relations bearing his name, which are fundamental for the thermodynamics of irreversible processes".*

1969 The prize was divided equally between:

BARTON, Sir DEREK H.R., Great Britain, Imperial College of Science and Technology, London, * 1918, and

HASSEL, ODD, Norway, Kjemisk Institutt, Oslo University, Oslo, * 1897, † 1981: *"for their contributions to the development of the concept of conformation and its application in chemistry".*

1970 LELOIR, LUIS F., Argentina, Institute for Biochemical Research, Buenos Aires, * 1906: *"for his discovery of sugar nucleotides and their role in the biosynthesis of carbohydrates".*

1971 HERZBERG, GERHARD, Canada, National Reseach Council of Canada, Ottawa, * 1904 (in Hamburg, Germany): *"for his contributions to the knowledge of electronic structure and geometry of molecules, particularly free radicals".*

1972 The prize was divided, one half being awarded to:

ANFINSEN, CHRISTIAN B., U.S.A., National Institutes of Health, Bethesda, Maryland, * 1916: *"for his work on ribonuclease, especially concerning the connection between the amino acid sequence and the biologically active conformation".*

and the other half jointly to:

MOORE, STANFORD, U.S.A., Rockefeller University, New York, N.Y., * 1913 † 1982, and

STEIN, WILLIAM H., U.S.A., Rockefeller University, New York, N.Y., * 1911, † 1980:

"for their contribution to the understanding of the connection between chemical structure and catalytic activity of the active centre of the ribonuclease molecule".

1973 The prize was divided equally between:

FISCHER, ERNST OTTO, Federal Republic of Germany, Technical University of Munich, Munich, * 1918, and

WILKINSON, Sir GEOFFREY, Great Britain, Imperial College, London, * 1921: *"for their pioneering work, performed independently, on the chemistry of the organometallic so called sandwich compounds".*

1974 FLORY, PAUL J., U.S.A., Stanford University, Stanford, * 1910: *"for his fundamental achievements, both theoretical and experimental, in the physical chemistry of the macromolecules".*

1975 The prize was divided equally between:

CORNFORTH, Sir JOHN WARCUP, Australia and Great Britain, University of Sussex, Brighton, * 1917: *"for his work on the stereochemistry of enzyme-catalyzed reactions"* and

John Warcup Cornforth

PRELOG, VLADIMIR, Switzerland, Eidgenössische Technische Hochschule, Zürich, * 1906 (Sarajevo, Bosnien): *"for his research into the stereochemistry of organic molecules and reactions".*

1976 LIPSCOMB Jr., WILLIAM N, U.S.A., Harvard University, Cambridge, Mass., * 1919: *"for his studies on the structure of boranes illuminating problems of chemical bonding".*

Herbert C Brown

1977 PRIGOGINE, ILYA, Belgium, Université Libre de Bruxelles, Brussells (University of Texas, U.S.A.), * 1917 (Moscow, Russia): *"for his contributions to non-equilibrium thermodynamics, particularly the theory of dissipative structures".*

1978 MITCHELL, PETER, Great Britain, Glynn Research Laboratories, Bodmin, * 1920: *"for his contribution to the understanding of biological energy transfer through the formulation of the chemiosmotic theory".*

1979 The prize was divided equally between:

BROWN, HERBERT C., U.S.A., Purdue University, West Lafayette, Indiana, * 1912 (London) and

WITTIG, GEORG, Germany, University of Heidelberg, Federal Republic of Germany, * 1897: *"for their development of the use of boron- and phosphourus-containing compounds, respectively, into important reagents in organic synthesis".*

1980 The prize was divided, one half being awarded to:

BERG, PAUL, U.S.A., Stanford University, Stanford, Calif., * 1926: *"for his fundamental studies of the biochemistry of nucleic acids, with particular regard to recombinant-DNA";*

and the other half jointly to;

GILBERT, WALTER, U.S.A., Biological Laboratories, Cambridge, Mass., * 1932 and

SANGER, FREDERICK, Great Britain, MRC Laboratory of Molecular Biology, Cambridge, * 1918: *"for their contributions concerning the determination of base sequences in nucleic acids".*

1981 The prize was awarded jointly to:

FUKUI, KENICHI, Japan, Kyoto University, Kyoto, Japan, * 1918 and

HOFFMANN, ROALD, U.S.A., Cornell University, Ithaca, N.Y., U.S.A., * 1937: *"for their theories, developed independently, concerning the course of chemical reactions".*

1982 KLUG, AARON, Great Britain, MRC Laboratory of Molecular Biology, Cambridge, Great Britain, * 1926: *for his development of crystallographic electron microscopy and his structural elucidation of biologically important nucleic acid-protein complexes".*

PHYSIOLOGY OR MEDICINE

1901 VON BEHRING, EMIL ADOLF, Germany, Marburg University, * 1854, † 1917: *"for his work on serum therapy, especially its application against diphteria, by which he has opened a new road in the domain of medical science and thereby placed in the hands of the physician a victorious weapon against illness and deaths".*

1902 ROSS, Sir RONALD, Great Britain, University College, Liverpool, * 1857 (in Almora, India), † 1932: *"for his work on malaria, by which he has shown how it enters the organism and thereby has laid the foundation for successful research on this disease and methods of combatting it".*

1903 FINSEN, NIELS RYBERG, Denmark, Finsen Medical Light Institute, Copenhagen, * 1860 (in Thorshavn, Faroe Islands), † 1904: *"in recognition of his contribution to the treatment of diseases, especially lapus vulgaris, with concentrated light radiation whereby he has opened a new avenue for medical science".*

1904 PAVLOV, IVAN PETROVIČ, Russia, Military Medical Academy, St. Petersburg (now Leningrad), * 1849, † 1936: *"in recognition of his work on the physiology of digestion, through which knowledge on vital aspects of the subject has been transformed and enlarged".*

1905 KOCH, ROBERT, Germany, Institut für Infektions-Krankheiten (Institute for Infectious Diseases), Berlin, * 1843, † 1910: *"for his investigations and discoveries in relation to tuberculosis".*

1906 The prize was awarded jointly to:

GOLGI, CAMILLIO, Italy, Pavia University, * 1843, † 1926; and

RAMON Y CAJAL, SANTIAGO, Spain, Madrid University, * 1852, † 1934: *"in recognition of their work on the structure of the nervous system".*

Emil Adolf von Behring

1907 LAVERAN, CHARLES LUIS ALPHONSE, France, Institut Pasteur, Paris, * 1845, † 1922: *"in recognition of his work on the role played by protozoa in causing diseases".*

1908 The prize was awarded jointly to:

MEČNIKOV, ILJA ILJIČ, Russia, Institut Pasteur, Paris, France, * 1845, † 1916; and

EHRLICH, PAUL, Germany, Goettingen University and Königliches Institut für experimentelle Therapie (Royal Institute for Experimental Therapy), Frankfort-on-the-Main, * 1854, † 1915: *"in recognition of their work on immunity".*

1909 KOCHER, EMIL THEODOR, Switzerland, Berne University, * 1841, † 1917: *for his work on the physiology, pathology and surgery of the thyroid gland".*

1910 KOSSEL, ALBRECHT, Germany, Heidelberg University, * 1853, † 1927: *"in recognition of the contributions to our knowledge of cell chemistry made through his work on proteins, including the nucleic substances".*

1911 GULLSTRAND, ALLVAR, Sweden, Uppsala University, * 1862, † 1930: *"for his work on the dioptrics of the eye".*

1912 CARREL, ALEXIS, France, Rockefeller Institute for Medical Research, New York, N.Y., * 1873, † 1944: *"in recognition of his work on vascular suture and the transplantation of blood-vessels and organs".*

1913 RICHET, CHARLES ROBERT, France, Sorbonne University, Paris, * 1850, † 1935: *"in recognition of his work on anaphylaxis".*

1914 BÀRÀNY, ROBERT, Hungary, Vienna University, * 1876 (in Vienna, Austria), † 1936: *"for his work on the physiology and pathology of the vestibular apparatus".*

1915 Reserved.

1916 The prize money for 1915 was allocated to the Special Fund of this prize section.

The prize for 1916: Reserved.

1917 The prize money for 1916 was allocated to the Special Fund of this prize section.

The prize for 1917: Reserved.

1918 The prize money for 1917 was allocated to the Special Fund of this prize section.

The prize for 1918: Reserved.

1919 The prize money for 1918 was allocated to the Special Fund of this prize section.

The prize for 1919: Reserved.

1920 The prize for 1919:

BORDET, JULES, Belgium, Brussels University, * 1870, † 1961: *"for his discoveries relating to immunity".*

The prize for 1920:

KROGH, SCHACK AUGUST STEEN-BERGER, Denmark, Copenhagen University, * 1874, † 1949: *"for his discovery of the capillary motor regulating mechanism".*

1921 Reserved.

1922 The prize money for 1921 was allocated to the Special Fund of this prize section.

The prize for 1922: Reserved.

1923 The prize for 1922 was divided equally between:

HILL, Sir ARCHIBALD VIVIAN, Great Britain, London University, * 1886, † 1977: *"for his discovery relating to the production of heat in the muscle";* and

MEYERHOF, OTTO FRITZ, Germany, Kiel University, * 1884, † 1951: *"for his discovery of the fixed relationship between the consumption of oxygen and the metabolism of lactid acid in the muscle".*

The prize for 1923 was awarded jointly to:

BANTING, Sir FREDERICK GRANT, Canada, Toronto University, * 1891, † 1941; and

MACLEOD, JOHN JAMES RICHARD, Canada, Toronto University, * 1876 (in Cluny, Scotland), † 1935: *"for the discovery of insulin".*

1924 EINTHOVEN, WILLEM, the Netherlands, Leyden University, * 1860 (in Semarang, Java, then Dutch East Indies), † 1927: *for his discovery of the mechanism of the electrocardiogram".*

1925 Reserved.

1926 The prize money for 1925 was allocated to the Special Fund of this prize section.

The prize for 1926: Reserved.

1927 The prize for 1926:

FIBIGER, JOHANNES ANDREAS GRIB, Denmark, Copenhagen University, * 1867, † 1928: *"for his discovery of the Spiroptera carcinoma".*

The prize for 1927:

WAGNER-JAUREGG, JULIUS, Austria, Vienna University, * 1857, † 1940: *"for his discovery of the therapeutic value of malaria inoculation in the treatment of dementia paralytica".*

1928 NICOLLE, CHARLES JULES HENRI, France, Institut Pasteur, Tunis, * 1866, † 1936: *"for his work on typhus".*

1929 The prize was divided equally between:

EIJKMAN, CHRISTIAAN, the Netherlands, Utrecht University, * 1858, † 1930: *"for his discovery of the antineuritic vitamin";* and

HOPKINS, Sir FREDERICK GOWLAND, Great Britain, Cambridge University, * 1861, † 1947: *"for his discovery of the growth-stimulating vitamins".*

1930 LANDSTEINER, KARL, Austria, Rockefeller Institute for Medical Research, New York, N.Y., U.S.A., * 1868, † 1943: *"for his discovery of human blood groups".*

1931 WARBURG, OTTO HEINRICH, Germany, Kaiser-Wilhelm-Institut (now Max-Planck-Institut) für Biologie, Berlin-Dahlem, * 1883, † 1970: *"for his discovery of the nature and mode of action of the respiratory enzyme".*

1932 The prize was awarded jointly to:

SHERRINGTON, Sir CHARLES SCOTT, Great Britain, Oxford University, * 1857, † 1952; and

ADRIAN, Lord EDGAR DOUGLAS, Great Britain, Cambridge University, * 1889, † 1977: *"for their discoveries regarding the functions of neurons".*

1933 MORGAN, THOMAS HUNT, U.S.A., California Institute of Technology, Pasadena, Calif., * 1866, † 1945: *"for his discoveries concerning the role played by the chromosome in heredity".*

1934 The prize was awarded jointly to:

WHIPPLE, GEORGE HOYT, U.S.A., Rochester University, Rochester, N.Y., * 1878, † 1976;

MINOT, GEORGE RICHARDS, U.S.A., Harvard University, Cambridge, Mass., * 1885, † 1950; and

MURPHY, WILLIAM PARRY, U.S.A., Harvard University, Cambridge, Mass., and Peter Brent Brigham Hospital, Boston, Mass., * 1892: *"for their discoveries concerning liver therapy in cases of anaemia".*

1935 SPEMANN, HANS, Germany, University of Freiburg im Breisgau, * 1869, † 1941: *"for his discovery of the organizer effect in embryonic development".*

Edgar Douglas Adrian

1936 The prize was awarded jointly to:

DALE, Sir HENRY HALLETT, Great Britain National Institute for Medical Research, London, * 1875, † 1968; and

LOEWI, OTTO, Austria, Graz University, * 1873 (in Frankfurt-on-the-Main, Germany), † 1961: *"for their discoveries relating to chemical transmission of nerve impulses".*

1937 SZENT-GYÖRGYI VON NAGYRAPOLT, ALBERT, Hungary, Szeged University, * 1893: *"for his discoveries in connection with the biological combustion processes, with special reference to vitamin C and the catalysis of fumaric acid".*

1938 Reserved.

1939 The prize for 1938:

HEYMANS, CORNEILLE JEAN FRANÇOIS, Belgium, Ghent University, * 1892, † 1968: *"for the discovery of the role played by the sinus and aortic mechanisms in the regulation of respiration".*

The prize for 1939:

DOMAGK, GERHARD, Germany, Munster University, * 1895, † 1964: *"for the discovery of the antibacterial effects of prontosil".* (Caused by the authorities of his country to decline the award, but later received the diploma and the medal.)

1940 The prize money was with 1/3 allocated to
–1942 the Main Fund and with 2/3 to the Special
Fund of this prize section.

1943 Reserved.

1944 The prize for 1943 was divided equally between:

DAM, HENRIK CARL PETER, Denmark, Polytechnic Institute, Copenhagen, * 1895, † 1976: *"for his discovery of vitamin K"*; and

DOISY, EDWARD ADELBERT, U.S.A., Saint Louis University, St. Louis, Mo., * 1893: *"for his discovery of the chemical nature of vitamin K"*.

The prize for 1944 was awarded jointly to:

ERLANGER; JOSEPH, U.S.A., Washington University, St. Louis, Mo., * 1874, † 1965; and

GASSER, HERBERT SPENCER, U.S.A., Rockefeller Institute for Medical Research, New York, N.Y., * 1888, † 1963: *"for their discoveries relating to the highly differentiated functions of single nerve fibres"*.

1945 The prize was awarded jointly to:

FLEMING, Sir ALEXANDER, Great Britain, London University, * 1881 (in Lochfield, Scotland), † 1955;

CHAIN, Sir ERNST BORIS, Great Britain, Oxford University, * 1906 (in Berlin, Germany), † 1979, and

FLOREY, Lord HOWARD WALTER, Great Britain, Oxford University, * 1898 (in Adelaide, Australia), † 1968: *"for the discovery of penicillin and its curative effect in various infectious diseases"*.

1946 MULLER, HERMANN JOSEPH, U.S.A., Indiana University, Bloomington, Indiana, * 1890, † 1967: *"for the discovery of the production of mutations by means of X-ray irradiation"*.

1947 The prize was divided, one half being awarded jointly to:

CORI, CARL FERDINAND, U.S.A., Washington University, St. Louis, Mo., * 1896 (in Prague, then Austria), and his wife

CORI, GERTY THERESA, née RADNITZ, U.S.A., Washington University, St. Louis, Mo., * 1986 (in Prague, then Austria) † 1957: *"for their discovery of the course of the catalytic conversion of glycogen"*.

the other half being awarded to:

Ernst Boris Chain

HOUSSAY, BERNARDO ALBERTO, Argentina, Instituto de Biologia y Medicina Experimental (Institute for Biology and Experimental Medicine), Buenos Aires, * 1887, † 1971: *"for his discovery of the part played by the hormone of the anterior pituitary lobe in the metabolism of sugar"*.

1948 MÜLLER, PAUL HERMANN, Switzerland, Laboratorium der Farben-Fabriken J.R. Geigy A.G. (Laboratory of the J.R. Geigy Dye-Factory Co.), Basel, * 1899, † 1965: *"for his discovery of the high efficiency of DDT as a contact poison against several arthropods"*.

1949 The prize was divided equally between:

HESS, WALTER RUDOLF, Switzerland, Zurich University, * 1881, † 1973: *"for his discovery of the functional organization of the interbrain as a coordinator of the activities of the internal organs"*; and

MONIZ, ANTONIO CAETANO DE ABREU FREIRE EGAS, Portugal, University of Lisbon, Neurological Institute, Lisbon, * 1874, † 1955: *"for his discovery of the therapeutic value of leucotomy in certain psychoses"*.

1950 The prize was awarded jointly to:

KENDALL, EDWARD CALVIN, U.S.A., Mayo Clinic, Rochester, Minn., * 1886, † 1972;

REICHSTEIN, TADEUS, Switzerland, Basel University, * 1897 (in Wloclawek, Poland); and

HENCH, PHILIP SHOWALTER, U.S.A., Mayo Clinic, Rochester, Minn., * 1896, † 1965: *"for their discoveries relating to the hormones of the adrenal cortex, their structure and biological effects"*.

1951 THEILER, MAX, Union of South Africa, Laboratories Division of Medicine and Public Health, Rockefeller Foundation, New York, N.Y., U.S.A., * 1899, † 1972: *"for his discoveries concerning yellow fever and how to combat it"*.

1952 WAKSMAN, SELMAN ABRAHAM, U.S.A., Rutgers University, New Brunswick, N.J., * 1888 (in Priluka, Ukraine, Russia), † 1973: *"for his discovery of streptomycin, the first antibiotic effective against tuberculosis"*.

1953 The prize was divided equally between:

KREBS, Sir HANS ADOLF, Great Britain, Sheffield University, * 1900 (in Hildesheim, Germany) † 1981: *"for his discovery of the citric acid cycle"*; and

LIPMANN, FRITZ ALBERT, U.S.A., Harvard Medical School and Massachusetts General Hospital, Boston, Mass., * 1899 (in Koenigsberg, then Germany): *"for his discovery of coenzyme A and its importance for intermediary metabolism"*.

1954 The prize was awarded jointly to:

ENDERS, JOHN FRANKLIN, U.S.A., Harvard Medical School, Boston, Mass.; Research Division of Infectious Diseases, Children's Medical Center, Boston, * 1897;

WELLER, THOMAS HUCKLE, U.S.A., Research Division of Infectious Diseases, Children's Medical Center, Boston, Mass., * 1915; and

ROBBINS, FREDERICK CHAPMAN, U.S.A., Western Reserve University, Cleveland, Ohio, * 1916: *"for their discovery of the ability of poliomyelitis viruses to grow in cultures of various types of tissue"*.

1955 THEORELL, AXEL HUGO THEODOR, Sweden, Nobel Medical Institute, Stockholm, * 1903: † 1982: *"for his discoveries* concerning the nature and mode of action of oxidation enzymes".

1956 The prize was awarded jointly to:

COURNAND, ANDRÉ FRÉDÉRIC, U.S.A., Cardio-Pulmonary Laboratory, Columbia University Division, Bellevue Hospital, New York, N.Y., * 1895 (in Paris, France);

FORSSMANN, WERNER, Germany, Mainz University and Bad Kreuznach, * 1904, † 1979, and

RICHARDS, Jr., DICKINSON W., U.S.A., Columbia University, New York, * 1895, † 1973: *"for their discoveries concerning heart catheterization and pathological changes in the circulatory system".*

André Frédéric Cournand

1957 BOVET, DANIEL, Italy, Instituto Superiore di Sanità (Chief Institute of Public Health), Rome, * 1907 (in Neuchâtel, Switzerland): *"for his discoveries relating to synthetic compounds that inhibit the action of certain body substances, and especially their action on the vascular system and the skeletal muscles".*

1958 The prize was divided, one half being awarded jointly to:

BEADLE, GEORGE WELLS, U.S.A., California Institute of Technology, Pasadena, Calif., * 1903; and

TATUM, EDWARD LAWRIE, U.S.A., Rockefeller Institute for Medical Research, New York, * 1909: *"for their discovery that genes act by regulating definite chemical events";*

and the other half to:

LEDERBERG, JOSHUA, U.S.A., Wisconsin University, Madison, Wisconsin, * 1925: *"for his discoveries concerning genetic recombination and the organization of the genetic material of bacteria".*

1959 The prize was awarded jointly to:

OCHOA, SEVERO, U.S.A., New York University, College of Medicine, New York, * 1905 (in Luarca, Spain); and

KORNBERG, ARTHUR, U.S.A., Stanford University, Stanford, Calif., * 1918: *"for their discovery of the mechanisms in the biological synthesis of ribonucleic acid and deoxyribonucleic acid".*

1960 The prize was awarded jointly to:

BURNET, Sir FRANK MACFARLANE, Australia, Walter and Eliza Hall Institute for Medical Research, Melbourne, * 1899; and

MEDAWAR, Sir PETER BRIAN, Great Britain, University College, London, * 1915: *"for discovery of acquired immunological tolerance".*

1961 VON BÉKÉSY, GEORG, U.S.A., Harvard University, Cambridge, Mass., *1899 (in Budapest), † 1972: *"for his discoveries of the physical mechanism of stimulation within the cochlea".*

1962 The prize was awarded jointly to:

CRICK, FRANCIS HARRY COMPTON, Great Britain, Institute of Molecular Biology, Cambridge, * 1916;

WATSON, JAMES DEWEY, U.S.A., Harvard University, Cambridge, Mass., *1928; and

WILKINS, MAURICE HUGH FREDERICK, Great Britain, University of London, *1916: *"for their discoveries concerning the molecular structure of nuclear acids and its significance for information transfer in living material".*

1963 The prize was awarded jointly to:

ECCLES, Sir JOHN CAREW, Australia, Australian National University, Canberra, * 1903;

HODGKIN, Sir ALAN LLOYD, Great Britain, Cambridge University, Cambridge, * 1914; and

HUXLEY, Sir ANDREW FIELDING, Great Britain, London University, * 1917: *"for their discoveries concerning the ionic mechanisms involved in excitation an inhibition*

in the peripheral and central portions of the nerve cell membrane".

1964 The prize was awarded jointly to:

BLOCH, KONRAD U.S.A., Harvard University, Cambridge, Mass., * 1912 (in Neisse, Germany); and

LYNEN, FEODOR, Germany, Max-Planck-Institut für Zellchemie, Munich, * 1911, † 1979: *"for their discoveries concerning the mechanism and regulation of the cholesterol and fatty acid metabolism".*

Frank MacFarlane Burnet

1965 The prize was awarded jointly to:

JACOB, FRANÇOIS, France, Institut Pasteur, Paris, * 1920;

LWOFF, ANDRÉ, France, Institut Pasteur, Paris, *1902; and

MONOD, JACQUES, France, Institut Pasteur, Paris, * 1910, † 1976: *"for their discoveries concerning genetic control of enzyme and virus synthesis".*

1966 The prize was divided equally between:

ROUS, PEYTON, U.S.A., Rockefeller University, New York, N.Y., * 1879, † 1970: *"for his discovery of tumorinducing viruses"*; and

HUGGINS, CHARLES BRENTON, U.S.A., Ben May Laboratory for Cancer Research, University of Chicago, Chicago, Ill., * 1901: *"for his discoveries concerning hormonal treatment of prostatic cancer"*.

Julius Axelrod

1967 The prize was awarded jointly to:

GRANIT, RAGNAR, Sweden, Karolinska institutet, Stockholm, * 1900 (in Helsinki, Finland);

HARTLINE, HALDAN KEFFER, U.S.A., The Rockefeller University, New York, N.Y., * 1903 † 1983; and

WALD, GEORGE, U.S.A., Harvard University, Cambridge, Mass., * 1906: *"for their discoveries concerning the primary physiological and chemical visual processes in the eye"*.

1968 The prize was awarded jointly to:

HOLLEY, ROBERT W., U.S.A., Cornell University, Ithaca, N.Y., * 1922;

KHORANA, HAR GOBIND, U.S.A., University of Wisconsin, Madison, Wis., * 1922 (in Raipur, India); and

NIRENBERG, MARSHALL W., U.S.A., National Institutes of Health, Bethesda, Md., * 1927: *"for their interpretation of the genetic code and its function in protein synthesis"*.

1969 The prize was awarded jointly to:

DELBRÜCK, MAX, U.S.A., California Institute of Technology, Pasadena, California, * 1906 (in Berlin, Germany), † 1981;

HERSHEY, ALFRED D., U.S.A., Carnegie Institution of Washington, Long Island, New York, * 1908; and

LURIA, SALVADOR E., U.S.A., Massachusetts Institute of Technology, Cambridge, Massachusetts, * 1912 (in Torino, Italy): *"for their discoveries concerning the replication mechanism and the genetic structure of viruses"*.

1970 The prize was awarded jointly to:

KATZ, Sir BERNARD, Great Britain, University College, London, * 1911;

VON EULER, ULF, Sweden, Karolinska institutet, Stockholm, * 1905 † 1983; and

AXELROD, JULIUS, U.S.A., National Institutes of Health, Bethesda, Maryland, * 1912: *"for their discoveries concerning the humoral transmittors in the nerve terminals and the mechanism for their storage, release and inactivation"*.

1971 SUTHERLAND, EARL W., JR., U.S.A., Vanderbilt University, Nashville, Tennessee, * 1915, † 1974: *"for his discoveries concerning the mechanisms of the action of hormones"*.

1972 The prize was awarded jointly to:

EDELMAN, GERALD M., U.S.A., Rockefeller University, New York, N.Y., * 1929; and

PORTER, RODNEY, R., Great Britain, University of Oxford, Oxford, * 1917: *"for their discoveries concerning the chemical structure of antibodies"*.

1973 The prize was awarded jointly to:

VON FRISCH, KARL, Federal Republic of Germany, Zoologisches Institut der Universität München, Munich, * 1886 (in Vienna, Austria) † 1982;

LORENZ, KONRAD, Austria, Österreichische Akademie der Wissenschaften, Institut für vergleichende Verhaltensforschung, Altenberg, * 1903; and

TINBERGEN, NIKOLAAS, Great Britain, Department of Zoology, University Museum, Oxford, * 1907 (in Hague, The Netherlands): *"for their discoveries concerning organization and elicitation of individual and social behaviour patterns"*.

1974 The prize was awarded jointly to:

CLAUDE, ALBERT, Belgium, Université Catholique de Louvain, Louvain, * 1899;

DE DUVE, CHRISTIAN, Belgium, The Rockefeller University, New York, * 1917; and

PALADE, GEORGE E., U.S.A., Yale University School of Medicine, New Haven, Connecticut, * 1912 (in Iasi, Roumania): *"for their discoveries concerning the structural and functional organization of the cell"*.

1975 The prize was awarded jointly to:

BALTIMORE, DAVID, U.S.A., Massachusetts Institute of Technology, Cambridge, Mass., * 1938, and

DULBECCO, RENATO, U.S.A., Imperial Cancer Research Fund Laboratory, London, * 1914 (in Catanzaro, Italy); and

Baruch S Blumberg

TEMIN, HOWARD MARTIN, U.S.A., University of Wisconsin, Madison, Wisconsin, * 1934: *"for their discoveries concerning the interaction between tumour viruses and the genetic material of the cell"*.

1976 The prize was awarded jointly to:

BLUMBERG, BARUCH S., U.S.A., The Institute for Cancer Research, Philadelphia, Pennsylvania, * 1925, and

GAJDUSEK, D. CARLETON, U.S.A., National Institutes of Health, Bethesda, Maryland, * 1923: *"for their discoveries concerning new mechanisms for the origin and dissemination of infectious diseases"*.

Werner Arber

1977 The prize was divided, one half being awarded jointly to:

GUILLEMIN, ROGER, U.S.A., The Salk Institute, San Diego, Calif., * 1924 (in Dijon, France); and

SCHALLY, ANDREW, U.S.A., Veterans Administration Hospital, New Orleans, Louis., * 1926 (in Wilno, Poland): *"for their discoveries concerning the peptide hormone production of the brain"*.

and the other half being awarded to:

YALOW, ROSALYN, U.S.A., Veterans Administration Hospital, Bronx, * 1921: *"for the development of radioimmunoassays of peptide hormones"*.

1978 The prize was awarded jointly to:

ARBER, WERNER, Switzerland, Biozentrum der Universität Basel, * 1929;

NATHANS, DANIEL, U.S.A., Johns Hopkins University School of Medicine, Baltimore, Maryland, * 1928; and

SMITH, HAMILTON O., Johns Hopkins University School of Medicine, Baltimore, Maryland, * 1931: *"for the discovery of restriction enzymes and their application to problems of molecular genetics"*.

1979 The prize was awarded jointly to:

CORMACK, ALLAN M., U.S.A., Tufts University, Medford, Mass., * 1924 (Johannesburg, South Africa) and

HOUNSFIELD, Sir GODFREY N., Great Britain, Central Research Laboratories, EMI, London, * 1919: *"for the development of computer assisted tomography"*.

Allan M Cormack

1980 The prize was awarded jointly to:

BENACERRAF, BARUJ, U.S.A., Harvard Medical School, Boston, Mass., * 1920 (Caracas, Venezuela);

DAUSSET, JEAN, France, Université de Paris, Laboratoire Immuno-Hématologie, Paris, * 1916 and

SNELL, GEORGE D., U.S.A., Jackson Laboratory, Bar Harbor, Maine, * 1903: *"for their*

discoveries concerning genetically determined structures on the cell surface that regulate immunological reactions"*.

1981 The prize was awarded by one half to:

SPERRY, ROGER W., U.S.A., California Institute of Technology, Pasadena, Calif., U.S.A., * 1913: *"for his discoveries concerning the functional specialization of the cerebral hemispheres"*, and

the other half to:

HUBEL, DAVID H., U.S.A., Harvard Medical School, Boston, Mass., U.S.A., * 1926;

WIESEL, TORSTEN N., Sweden, Harvard Medical School, Boston, Mass., U.S.A., * 1924: *"for their discoveries concerning information processing in the visual system"*.

1982 The prize was awarded jointly to:

BERGSTRÖM, SUNE, Sweden, Karolinska institutet, Stockholm, Sweden, * 1916;

SAMUELSSON, BENGT I., Sweden, Karolinska institutet, Stockholm, Sweden, * 1934, and

VANE, JOHN R., Great Britain, The Wellcome Research Laboratories, Beckenham, Great Britain, * 1927: *"for their discoveries concerning prostaglandins and related biologically active substances"*.

Baruj Benacerraf

1901 SULLY PRUDHOMME (pen-name of PRUDHOMME, RENÉ FRANÇOIS ARMAND), France, * 1839, † 1907: *"in special recognition of his poetic composition, which gives evidence of lofty idealism, artistic perfection and a rare combination of the qualities of both heart and intellect"*.

1902 MOMMSEN, CHRISTIAN MATTHIAS THEODOR, Germany, * 1817 (in Garding, Sleswick, then Denmark), † 1903: *"the greatest living master of the art of historical writing, with special reference to his monumental work, A history of Rome"*.

1903 BJØRNSON, BJØRNSTJERNE MARTINUS, Norway, * 1832, † 1910: *"as a tribute to his noble, magnificent and versatile poetry, which has always been distinguished by both the freshness of its inspiration and the rare purity of its spirit"*.

1904 The prize was divided equally between:

MISTRAL, FRÉDÉRIC, France, * 1830, † 1914: *"in recognition of the fresh originality and true inspiration of his poetic production, which faithfully reflects the natural scenery and native spirit of his people, and, in addition, his significant work as a Provençal philologist"*; and

ECHEGARAY Y EIZAGUIRRE, JOSÉ, Spain, * 1833, † 1916: *"in recognition of the numerous and brilliant compositions which, in an individual and original manner, have revived the great traditions of the Spanish drama"*.

1905 SIENKIEWICZ, HENRYK, Poland, * 1846, † 1916: *"because of his outstanding merits as an epic writer"*.

1906 CARDUCCI, GIOSUÈ, Italy, * 1835, † 1907: *"not only in consideration of his deep learning and critical reseach, but above all as a tribute to the creative energy, freshness of style, and lyrical force which characterize his poetic masterpieces"*.

1907 KIPLING, RUDYARD, Great Britain, * 1865 (in Bombay, Br. India), † 1936: *"in consideration of the power of observation, originality of imagination, virility of ideas and remarkable talent for narration which characterize the creations of this world-famous author"*.

1908 EUCKEN, RUDOLF CHRISTOPH, Germany, * 1846, † 1926: *"in recognition of his earnest search for truth, his penetrating power of thought, his wide range of vision, and the warmth and strength in presentation with which in his numerous works he has vindicated and developed and idealistic philosophy of life"*.

1909 LAGERLÖF, SELMA OTTOLIANA LOVISA, Sweden, * 1858, † 1940: *"in appreciation of the lofty idealism, vivid imagination and spiritual perception that characterize her writings"*.

Björnstjerne Martinus Björnson

1910 HEYSE, PAUL JOHANN LUDWIG, Germany, * 1830, † 1914: *"as a tribute to the consummate artistry, permeated with idealism, which he has demonstrated during his long productive career as a lyric poet, dramatist, novelist and writer of world-renowned short stories"*.

1911 MAETERLINCK, Count, MAURICE (MOORIS) POLIDORE MARIE BERNHARD, Belgium, * 1862, † 1949: *"in appreciation of his many-sided literary activities, and especially of his dramatic works, which are distinguished by a wealth of imagination and by a poetic fancy, which reveals, sometimes in the guise of a fairy tale, a deep inspiration, while in a mysterious way the appeal to the readers' own feelings and stimulate their imaginations"*.

1912 HAUPTMANN, GERHARD JOHANN ROBERT, Germany, * 1862, † 1946: *"primarily in recognition of his fruitful, varied and outstanding production in the realm of dramatic art"*.

1913 TAGORE, RABINDRANATH, India, * 1861, † 1941: *"because of his profoundly sensitive, fresh and beautiful verse, by which, with consummate skill, he has made his poetic thought, expressed in his own English works, a part of the literature of the West"*,

1914 Reserved.

1915 The prize money for 1914 was allocated to the Special Fund of this prize section.

The prize for 1915: Reserved.

1916 The prize for 1915:

ROLLAND, ROMAIN, France, * 1866, † 1944: *"as a tribute to the lofty idealism of his literary production and to the sympathy and love of truth with which he has described different types of human beings"*.

The prize for 1916:

VON HEIDENSTAM, CARL GUSTAF VERNER, Sweden, * 1859, † 1940: *"in recognition of his significance as the leading representative of a new era in our literature"*.

1917 The prize was divided equally between:

GJELLERUP, KARL ADOLPH, Denmark, * 1857, † 1919: *for his varied and rich poetry, which is inspired by lofty ideals;* and

PONTOPPIDAN, HENRIK, Denmark, * 1857, † 1943: *"for his authentic descriptions of present-day life in Denmark"*.

1918 Reserved.

1919 The prize money for 1918 was allocated to the Special Fund of this prize section.

The prize for 1919: Reserved.

1920 The prize for 1919:

SPITTELER, CARL FRIEDRICH GEORG, Switzerland, * 1845, † 1924: *in special appreciation of his epic, Olympian Spring"*.

The prize for 1920:

HAMSUN, KNUT PEDERSEN, Norway, * 1859, †1952: "for his monumental work, Growth of the Soil".

1921 ANATOLE FRANCE (pen-name of THIBAULT, JACQUES ANATOLE), France, * 1844, † 1924: in recognition of his brilliant literary achievements, characterized as they are by a nobility of style, a profound human sympathy, grace, and a true Gallic temperament".

Anatole France

1922 BENAVENTE, JACINTO, Spain, * 1866, † 1954: *for the happy manner in which he has continued the illustrious traditions of the Spanish drama".*

1923 YEATS, WILLIAM BUTLER, Ireland, * 1865, † 1939: *for his always inspired poetry, which in a highly artistic form gives expression to the spirit of a whole nation".*

1924 REYMONT (pen-name of REYMENT), WLADYSLAW STANISLAW, Poland, * 1868, † 1925: *"for his great national epic, The Peasants".*

1925 Reserved.

1926 The prize for 1925:

SHAW, GEORGE BERNARD, Great Britain, * 1856 (in Dublin, Ireland), † 1950: *for his work which is marked by both idealism and humanity, its stimulating satire often being infused with a singular poetic beauty".*

The prize for 1926: Reserved.

1927 The prize for 1926:

GRAZIA DELEDDA (pen-name of MADESANI, GRAZIA, née DELEDDA), Italy, * 1871 (in Nuoro, Sardinia), † 1936: *"for her idealistically inspired writings which with plastic clarity picture the life on her native island and with depth and sympathy deal with human problems in general".*

The prize for 1927: Reserved.

1928 The prize for 1927:

BERGSON, HENRI, France, * 1859, † 1941: *"in recognition of his rich and vitalizing ideas and the brilliant skill with which they have been presented".*

The prize for 1928:

UNDSET, SIGRID, Norway, * 1882 (in Kalundborg, Denmark), † 1949: *"principally for her powerful descriptions of Northern life during the Middle Ages".*

1929 MANN, THOMAS, Germany, * 1875, † 1955: *"principally for his great novel, Buddenbrooks, which has won steadily increased recognition as one of the classic works of contemporary literature".*

1930 LEWIS, SINCLAIR, U.S.A., * 1885, † 1951: *"for his vigorous and graphic art of description and his ability to create, with wit and humour, new types of characters".*

1931 KARLFELDT, ERIK AXEL, Sweden, * 1864, † 1931: *"The poetry of Erik Axel Karlfeldt".*

1932 GALSWORTHY, JOHN, Great Britain, * 1867, † 1933: *"for his distinguished art of narration which takes its highest form in The Forsyte Saga".*

1933 BUNIN, IVAN ALEKSEJEVIČ, stateless domicile in France, * 1870 (in Voronež, Russia), † 1953: *"for the strict artistry with which he has carried on the classic Russian traditions in prose writing".*

1934 PIRANDELLO, LUIGI, Italy, * 1867, † 1936: *"for his bold and ingenious revival of dramatic and scenic art".*

Jacinto Benavente

1935 Reserved.

1936 The prize money for 1935 was with 1/3 allocated to the Main Fund and with 2/3 to the Special Fund of this prize section.

The prize for 1936:

O'NEILL, EUGENE GLADSTONE, U.S.A., * 1888, † 1953: *for the power, honesty and deep-felt emotions of his dramatic works, which embody an original concept of tragedy".*

1937 MARTIN DU GARD, ROGER, France, * 1881, † 1958: *"for the artistic power and truth with which he has depicted human conflict as well as some fundamental aspects of contemporary life in his novelcycle* Les Thibault".

1938 PEARL BUCK (pen-name of WALSH, PEARL, née SYDENSTRICKER), U.S.A., * 1892, † 1973: *"for her rich and truly epic descriptions of peasant life in China and for her biographical masterpieces".*

1939 SILLANPÄÄ, FRANS EEMIL, Finland, * 1888, † 1964: *"for his deep understanding of his country's peasantry and the exquisite art with which he has portrayed their way of life and their relationship with Nature".*

Pearl Buck

1940 The prize money was with 1/3 allocated to
–1943 the Main Fund and with 2/3 to the Special
Fund of this prize section.

1944 JENSEN, JOHANNES VILHELM, Denmark, * 1873, † 1950: *"for the rare strength and fertility of his poetic imagination with which is combined an intellectual curiosity of wide scope and a bold, freshly creative style".*

1945 GABRIELA MISTRAL (pen-name of GODOY Y ALCAYAGA, LUCILA), Chile, * 1889, † 1957: *"for her lyric poetry which, inspired by powerful emotions, has made her name a symbol of the idealistic aspirations of the entire Latin American world".*

1946 HESSE, HERMANN, Switzerland, * 1877 (in Calw, Wurttemberg, Germany), † 1962: *"for his inspired writings which, while growing in boldness and penetration, exemplify the classical humanitarian ideals and high quality of style".*

1947 GIDE, ANDRÉ PAUL GUILLAUME, France, * 1869, † 1951: *"for his comprehensive and artistically significant writings, in which human problems and conditions have been presented with a fearless love of truth and keen psychological insight".*

1948 ELIOT, THOMAS STEARNS, Great Britain, * 1888 (in S:t Louis, Mo., U.S.A.), † 1965: *"for his outstanding, pioneer contribution to present-day poetry".*

1949 Reserved.

1950 The prize for 1949:

FAULKNER, WILLIAM, U.S.A., * 1897, † 1962: *"for his powerful and artistically unique contribution to the modern American novel".*

The prize for 1950:

RUSSELL, Earl (BERTRAND ARTHUR WILLIAM), Great Britain, * 1872, † 1970: *"in recognition of his varied and significant writings in which he champions humanitarian ideals and freedom of thought".*

1951 LAGERKVIST, PÄR FABIAN, Sweden, * 1891, † 1974: *"for the artistic vigour and true independence of mind with which he endeavours in his poetry to find answers to the eternal questions confronting mankind".*

1952 MAURIAC, FRANÇOIS, France, * 1885, † 1970: *"for the deep spiritual insight and the artistic intensity with which he has in his novels penetrated the drama of human life".*

1953 CHURCHILL, Sir WINSTON LEONARD SPENCER, Great Britain, * 1874, † 1965: *"for his mastery of historical and biographical description as well as for brilliant oratory in defending exalted human values".*

1954 HEMINGWAY, ERNEST MILLER, U.S.A., * 1898, † 1961: *"for his mastery of the art of narrative, most recently demonstrated in* The Old Man and the Sea, *and for the influence that he has exerted on contemporary style".*

1955 LAXNESS, HALLDÓR, KILJAN, Iceland, * 1902: *for his vivid epic power which has renewed the great narrative art of Iceland".*

1956 JIMÉNEZ, JUAN RAMÓN, Spain (domicile in Puerto Rico, U.S.A.), * 1881, † 1958: *"for his lyrical poetry, which in Spanish language constitutes an example of high spirit and artistical purity".*

1957 CAMUS, ALBERT, France, * 1913 (in Mondovi, Algeria), † 1960: *"for his important literary production, which with clearsighted earnestness illuminates the problems of the human conscience in our times".*

1958 PASTERNAK, BORIS LEONIDOVIČ, USSR, * 1890, † 1960: *for his important achievement both in contemporary lyrical poetry and in the field of the great Russian epic tradition".* (Declined the prize).

1959 QUASIMODO, SALVATORE, Italy, * 1901, † 1968: *"for his lyrical poetry, which with classical fire expresses the tragic experience of life in our own times".*

Albert Camus

1960 SAINT-JOHN PERSE (pen-name of LÉGER, ALEXIS), France, * 1887 (on Guadelope Island), † 1975: *"for the soaring flight and the evocative imagery of his poetry which in a visionary fashion reflects the conditions of our time".*

1961 ANDRIĆ, IVO, Yugoslavia, * 1892 (in Travnik, Bosnia), † 1975: *"for the epic force with which he has traced themes and depicted human destinies drawn from the history of his country".*

1962 STEINBECK, JOHN, U.S.A., * 1902, † 1968: *"for his realistic and imaginative writings, combining as they do sympathetic humour and keen social perception".*

1963 SEFERIS, GIORGOS (pen-name of

SEFERIADIS, GIORGOS), Greece, * 1900 (in Smyrna, Turkey), † 1971: *"for his eminent lyrical writing, inspired by a deep feeling for the Hellenic world of culture"*.

1964 SARTRE, JEAN-PAUL, France, * 1905, † 1980: *"for his work which, rich in ideas and filled with the spirit of freedom and the quest for truth, has exerted a far-reaching influence on our age"*. (Declined the prize).

1965 ŠOLOCHOV, MICHAIL ALEKSANDRO-VIČ, USSR, * 1905: *"for the artistic power and integrity with which, in his epic of the Don, he has given expression to a historic phase in the life of the Russian people"*.

1966 The prize was divided equally between:

AGNON, SHMUEL YOSEF, Israel, * 1888, † 1970: *"for his profoundly characteristic narrative art with motifs from the life of the Jewish people"*; and

SACHS, NELLY, * 1891 in Germany, domiciled in Sweden since 1940, † 1970: *"for her outstanding lyrical and dramatic writing, which interprets Israel's destiny with touching strength"*.

1967 ASTURIAS, MIGUEL ANGEL, Guatemala, * 1899, † 1974: *"for his vivid literary achievement, deep-rooted in the national traits and traditions of Indian peoples of Latin America"*.

Shmuel Yosef Agnon

Heinrich Böll

1968 KAWABATA, YASUNARI, Japan, * 1899, † 1972: *"for his narrative mastery, which with great sensibility expresses the essence of the Japanese mind"*.

1969 BECKETT, SAMUEL, Ireland, * 1906: *"for his writing, which – in new forms for the novel and drama – in the destitution of modern man acquires its elevation"*.

1970 SOLSJENITSYN, ALEXANDER, USSR, * 1918: *"for the ethical force with which he has pursued the indispensable traditions of Russian literature"*.

1971 NERUDA, PABLO, Chile, * 1904, † 1973: *"for a poetry that with the action of an elemental force brings alive a continent's destiny and dreams"*.

1972 BÖLL, HEINRICH, Federal Republic of Germany, * 1917: *"for his writing which through its combination of a broad perspective on his time and a sensitive skill in characterization has contributed to a renewal of German literature"*.

1973 WHITE, PATRICK, Australia, * 1912 (in London, Great Britain): *"for an epic and psychological narrative art which has introduced a new continent into literature"*.

1974 The prize was divided equally between:

JOHNSON, EYVIND, Sweden, * 1900, † 1976: *"for a narrative art, far-seeing in lands*

and ages, in the service of freedom"*; and

MARTINSON, HARRY, Sweden, * 1904, † 1978: *"for writings that catch the dewdrop and reflect the cosmos"*.

1975 MONTALE, EUGENIO, Italy, * 1896: *"for his distinctive poetry which, with great artistic sensitivity, has interpreted human values under the sign of an outlook on life with no illusions"*.

1976 BELLOW, SAUL, U.S.A., * 1915: *"for the human understanding and subtle analysis of contemporary culture that are combined in his work"*.

Saul Bellow

1977 ALEIXANDRE, VICENTE, Spain, * 1898: *"for a creative poetic writing which illuminates man's condition in the cosmos and in present-day society, at the same time representing the great renewal of the traditions of Spanish poetry between the wars"*.

1978 SINGER, ISAAC BASHEVIS, U.S.A., * 1904 (in Radzymin, Poland): *"for his impassioned narrative art which, with roots in a Polish-Jewish cultural tradition, brings universal human conditions to life"*.

1979 ELYTIS, ODYSSEUS (pen-name of AL-EPOUDHELIS, ODYSSEUS), Greece, * 1911: *"for his poetry, which, against the background of Greek tradition, depicts with sensuous strength and intellectual clear-sightedness modern man's struggle for freedom and creativeness"*.

Gabriel García Márquez

1980 MIŁOSZ, CZESŁAW, U.S.A., and Poland, University of California, Berkeley, * 1911 (Seteiniai, Lituania): *"who with uncompromising clear-sightedness voices man's exposed condition in a world of severe conflicts".*

1981 CANETTI, ELIAS, Great Britain, * 1905: *"for writings marked by a broad outlook, a wealth of ideas and artistic power".*

1982 GARCIA MARQUEZ, GABRIEL, Colombia, * 1928: *"for his novels and short stories, in which the fantastic and the realistic are combined in a richly composed world of imagination, reflecting a continent's life and conflicts".*

PEACE

1901 The prize was divided between:

DUNANT, JEAN HENRI, Switzerland, Founder International Committee of the Red Cross (Comité International de la Croix-Rouge), Geneva, Originator Geneva Convention (Convention de Genève), * 1828, † 1910; and

PASSY, FRÉDÉRIC, France, Founder and President first French peace society (Ligue internationale et permanente de la paix; since 1889 called Société Française pour l'arbitrage entre nations), * 1822, † 1912.

1902 The prize was divided equally between:

DUCOMMUN, ÉLIE, Switzerland, Honorary Secretary Permanent International Peace Bureau (Bureau International Permanet de la Paix), Berne, * 1833, † 1906; and

GOBAT, CHARLES ALBERT, Switzerland, Secretary General Inter-Parliamentary Union (Bureau interparlementaire), Berne, Honorary Secretary Permanent International Peace Bureau (Bureau International Permanent de la Paix), Berne, * 1843, † 1914.

1903 CREMER, Sir WILLIAM RANDAL, Great Britain, Member British Parliament, Secretary International Arbitration League, * 1838, † 1908.

1904 INSTITUT DE DROIT INTERNATIONAL (INSTITUTE OF INTERNATIONAL LAW), Ghent, scientific society, founded 1873.

1905 VON SUTTNER, Baroness, BERTHA SOPHIE FELICITA, née Countess KINSKY von CHINIC und TETTAU, Austria, Writer, Hon., President Permanent International Peace Bureau (Bureau International Permanent de la Paix), Berne, Author "Lay Down Your Arms", * 1843 (in Prague, then Austria), † 1914.

1906 ROOSEVELT, THEODORE, U.S.A., President United States of America, Collaborator, various peace treaties, * 1858, † 1919.

1907 The prize was divided equally between:

MONETA, ERNESTO TEODORO, Italy, President Lombard League of Peace (Società internazionale per la pace: Unione Lombarda), * 1833, † 1918; and

RENAULT, LOUIS, France, Professor International Law, Sorbonne University, Paris, * 1843, † 1918.

1908 The prize was divided equally between:

ARNOLDSON, KLAS PONTUS, Sweden, Writer, formerly Member Swedish Parliament, Founder Swedish Peace and Arbitration League (Svenska freds- och skiljedomsföreningen), * 1844, † 1916; and

BAJER, FREDRIK, Denmark, Member Danish Parliament, Honorary President Permanent International Peace Bureau (Bureau International Permanent de la Paix), Berne, * 1837, † 1922.

1909 The prize was divided equally between:

Klas Pontus Arnoldson

BEERNAERT, AUGUSTE MARIE FRANÇOIS, Belgium, ex-Prime Minister, Member Belgian Parliament, Member Cour Internationale d'Arbitrage (International Court of Arbitration) at the Hague, * 1829, † 1912; and

D'ESTOURNELLES DE CONSTANT, PAUL HENRI BENJAMIN BALLUET, Baron DE CONSTANT DE REBECQUE, France, Member French Parliament (Sénateur), Founder and President French parliamentary group for voluntary arbitration (Groupe parlementaire de l'arbitrage international), Founder Comité de défense des intérêts nationaux et de conciliation internationale (Committee for the defense of national interests and international conciliation), * 1852, † 1924.

1910 BUREAU INTERNATIONAL PERMANENT DE LA PAIX (PERMANENT INTERNATIONAL PEACE BUREAU), Berne, founded 1891.

1911 The prize was divided equally between

ASSER, TOBIAS MICHAEL CAREL, the Netherlands, Prime Minister, Member Privy Council, Originator International Conferences of Private Law (Conférences de Droit international privé) at the Hague, * 1838, † 1913; and

FRIED ALFRED HERMANN, Austria, Journalist, Founder *"Die Friedenswarte"*, a peace publication, * 1864, † 1921.

1912 Reserved.

1913 The prize for 1912:

ROOT, ELIHU, U.S.A., i.a. ex-Secretary of State, Originator various treaties of arbitration, * 1845, † 1937.

The prize for 1913:

LA FONTAINE, HENRI, Belgium, Member Belgian Parliament (Sénateur), President Permanent International Peace Bureau (Bureau International Permanent de la Paix), Berne, * 1854, † 1943.

1914 Reserved.

1915 The prize money for 1914 was allocated to the Special Fund of the prize section.

The prize for 1915: Reserved.

1916 The prize money for 1915 was allocated to the Special Fund of this prize section.

The prize for 1916: Reserved.

Joseph Chamberlain

1917 The prize money for 1916 was allocated to the Special Fund of this prize section.

The prize for 1917:

COMITÉ INTERNATIONAL DE LA CROIX-ROUGE (INTERNATIONAL COMMITTEE OF THE RED CROSS), Geneva, founded 1863.

1918 Reserved.

1919 The prize money for 1918 was allocated to the Special Fund of this prize section.

The prize for 1919: Reserved.

1920 The prize for 1919:

WILSON, THOMAS WOODROW, U.S.A., President United States of America, Founder of Société des Nations (the League of Nations), * 1856, † 1924.

The prize for 1920:

BOURGEOIS, LÉON VICTOR AUGUSTE, France, i.a. ex-Secretary of State, President French Parliament (Sénat), President Conseil de la Société des Nations (Council of the League of Nations), * 1851, † 1925.

1921 The prize was divided equally between:

BRANTING, KARL HJALMAR, Sweden, Prime Minister, Swedish Delegate Conseil de la Société des Nations (Council of the League of Nations), * 1860, † 1925; and

LANGE, CHRISTIAN LOUIS, Norway, Secretary General Inter-Parliamentary Union (Bureau interparlementaire), Brussels, * 1869, † 1938.

1922 NANSEN, FRIDTJOF, Norway, Scientist, Explorer, Norweigian Delegate Société des Nations (League of Nations), Originator "Nansen passports" (for refugees), * 1861, † 1930.

1923 Reserved.

1924 The prize money for 1923 was allocated to the Special Fund of this section.

The prize for 1924: Reserved.

1925 The prize money for 1924 was allocated to the Special Fund of this prize section.

The prize for 1925: Reserved.

1926 The prize for 1925 was awarded jointly to:

CHAMBERLAIN, JOSEPH, Sir Austen, Great Britain, Foreign Secretary, Part-orginator Locarno Pact, * 1863, † 1937; and

DAWES, CHARLES GATES, U.S.A., Vice-President of United States of America, Chairman Allied Reparation Commission (Originator "Dawes Plan"), * 1865, † 1951.

The prize for 1926 was awarded jointly to:

BRIAND, ARISTIDE, France, Foreign Minister, Part-originator Locarno Pact, Briand-Kellogg Pact, * 1862, † 1932; and

Jane Addams

STRESEMANN, GUSTAV, Germany, ex-Lord High Chancellor (Reichskanzler), Foreign Minister, Part-originator Locarno Pact, * 1878, † 1929.

1927 The prize was divided equally between:

BUISSON, FERDINAND, France, formerly Professor Sorbonne University, Paris, Founder and President Ligue des Droits de l'Homme (League for Human Rights), * 1841, † 1932; and

QUIDDE, LUDWIG, Germany, Professor Berlin University, Member German Parliament, Participant various peace conferences, * 1858, † 1941

1928 Reserved.

1929 The prize money for 1928 was allocated to the Special Fund of this prize section.

The prize for 1929: Reserved.

1930 The prize for 1929

KELLOGG, FRANK BILLINGS, U.S.A., ex-Secretary of State, Part-originator Briand-Kellogg Pact, * 1856, † 1937.

The prize for 1930:

SÖDERBLOM, LARS OLOF NATHAN (JONATHAN), Sweden, Archbishop, Leader in the ecumenical movement, * 1866, † 1931.

1931 The prize was divided equally between:

ADDAMS, JANE, U.S.A., Sociologist, International President Women's International League for Peace and Freedom, * 1860, † 1935; and

Norman Angell

BUTLER, NICHOLAS MURRAY, U.S.A., President Columbia University, Promoter Briand-Kellogg Pact, * 1862, † 1947.

1932 Reserved.

1933 The prize money for 1932 was allocated to the Special Fund of this prize section.

The prize for 1933: Reserved.

1934 The prize for 1933:

ANGELL (RALPH LANE), Sir NORMAN, Great Britain, Writer, Member Commission Exécutive de la Société des Nations (Executive Committee of the League of Nations) and of National Peace Council, Author *"The Great Illusion"*, * 1874, † 1967.

The prize for 1934:

HENDERSON, ARTHUR, Great Britain, ex-Foreign Secretary, President Disarmament Conference 1932, * 1863, † 1935.

1935 Reserved.

1936 The prize for 1935:

VON OSSIETZKY, CARL, Germany, Journalist (i.a. "die Weltbühne"), Pacifist, * 1889, † 1938.

The prize for 1936:

SAAVEDRA LAMAS, CARLOS, Argentina, Secretary of State, President Société des Nations (League of Nations), Mediator in a conflict between Paraguay and Bolivia, * 1878, † 1959.

1937 CECIL OF CHELWOOD, Viscount, (Lord EDGAR ALGERNON ROBERT GASCOYNE CECIL), Great Britain, Writer, i.a. ex-Lord Privy Seal, Founder and President International Peace Campaign (Rassemblement Universel pour la Paix), * 1864, † 1958.

1938 OFFICE INTERNATIONAL NANSEN POUR LES RÉFUGIÉS (NANSEN INTERNATIONAL OFFICE FOR REFUGEES), Geneva, an international relief organization, started by Fridtjof Nansen, 1921.

1939 The prize money has been allocated with 1/3
–1942 to the Main Fund and with 2/3 to the Special Fund of this prize section.

1943 Reserved.

1944 The prize money for 1943 was allocated with 1/3 to the Main Fund and with 2/3 to the Special Fund of this prize section.

The prize for 1944: Reserved.

Cecil of Chelwood

Emily Greene Balch

1945 The prize for 1944:

COMITÉ INTERNATIONAL DE LA CROIX-ROUGE (INTERNATIONAL COMMITTEE OF THE RED CROSS), Geneva, founded 1863.

The prize for 1945:

HULL, CORDELL, U.S.A., ex-Secretary of State, Prominent part-taker in originating the United Nations, * 1871, † 1955.

1946 The prize was divided equally between:

BALCH, EMILY GREENE, U.S.A., formerly Professor of History and Sociology, Honorary International President Women's International League for Peace and Freedom, * 1867, † 1961; and

MOTT, JOHN RALEIGH, U.S.A., Chairman International Missionary Council, President World Alliance of Young Men's Christian Associations, * 1865, † 1955.

1947 The prize was awarded jointly to:

THE FRIENDS SERVICE COUNCIL (The Quakers), London, founded 1647; and

THE AMERICAN FRIENDS SERVICE COMMITTEE (The Quakers), Washington, first official meeting 1672.

1948 Reserved.

1949 The prize money for 1948 was allocated with 1/3 to the Main Fund and with 2/3 to the Special Fund of this prize section.

The prize for 1949:

BOYD ORR OF BRECHIN, Lord, JOHN, Great Britain, Physician, Alimentary Politician, Prominent organizer and Director General Food and Agricultural Organization, President National Peace Council and World Union of Peace Organizations, * 1880 (in Kilmaurs, Scotland), † 1971.

1950 BUNCHE, RALPH, U.S.A., Professor Harvard University, Cambridge, Mass., Director div. of Trusteeship U.N., Acting Mediator in Palestine 1948, * 1904, † 1971.

1951 JOUHAUX, LÉON, France, President Trade Union Confederation, "C.G.T.-Force Ouvrière". President Conseil National économique and International Committee of the European Council, Vice President International Confederation of Free Trade Unions, Vice President Fédération Syndicale Mondiale, Member Council of I.L.O. (International Labour Organization), Delegate U.N., * 1879, † 1954.

1952 Reserved.

1953 The prize for 1952:

SCHWEITZER, ALBERT, France, Missionary Surgeon, Founder Lambaréné Hospital (République du Gabon), * 1875 (in Kaysersberg, Alsace, then Germany), † 1965.

The prize for 1953:

MARSHALL, GEORGE CATLETT, U.S.A., General, President American Red Cross, ex-Secretary of State and of Defense, Delegate U.N., Originator "Marshall Plan", * 1880, † 1959.

1954 Reserved.

1955 The prize for 1954:

OFFICE OF THE UNITED NATIONS HIGH COMMISSIONER FOR REFUGEES, Geneva, an international relief organization, founded by U.N. in 1951.

The prize for 1955: Reserved.

1956 The prize money for 1955 was allocated with 1/3 to the Main Fund and with 2/3 to the Special Fund of this prize section.

The prize for 1956: Reserved.

1957 The prize money for 1956 was allocated with 1/3 to the Main Fund and with 2/3 to the Special Fund of this prize section.

The prize for 1957:

PEARSON, LESTER BOWLES, Canada, former Secretary of State, Foreign Department in Canada, President 7th Session of the United Nations General Assembly, * 1897, † 1972.

1958 PIRE, GEORGES, Belgium, Father of the Dominican Order, Leader of the relief organization for refugees "l'Europe du Coeur au Service du Monde", * 1910, † 1969.

René Cassin

1959 NOEL-BAKER, PHILIP J., Great Britain, Member of Parliament, lifelong ardent worker for international peace and co-operation, * 1889 † 1982.

1960 Reserved.

1961 The prize for 1960:

LUTULI, ALBERT JOHN, South Africa, President of the African National Congress in S.A., * 1898 (in Southern Rhodesia), † 1967.

The prize for 1961:

HAMMARSKJÖLD, DAG HJALMAR AGNE CARL, p.m., Sweden, Secretary General of the U.N., * 1905. † 1961.

1962 Reserved.

1963 The prize for 1962:

PAULING, LINUS CARL, U.S.A., California Institute of Technology, Pasadena, Calif., * 1901.

The prize for 1963 was divided equally between:

COMITÉ INTERNATIONAL DE LA CROIX-ROUGE (INTERNATIONAL COMMITTEE OF THE RED CROSS), Geneva, founded 1863; and

LIGUE DES SOCIÉTÉS DE LA CROIX-ROUGE (LEAGUE OF RED CROSS SOCIETIES), Geneva.

1964 KING JR., MARTIN LUTHER, U.S.A., leader of "Southern Christian Leadership Conference", * 1929, † 1968.

1965 UNITED NATIONS CHILDREN'S FUND (UNICEF), New York, founded by U.N. in 1946.

1966 Reserved.

1967 The prize money for 1966 was allocated with 1/3 to the Main Fund and with 2/3 to the Special Fund of this prize section.

The prize for 1967: Reserved.

1968 The prize money for 1967 was allocated with 1/3 to the Main Fund and with 2/3 to the Special Fund of this prize section.

The prize for 1968:

CASSIN, RENÉ, France, President of the European Court for Human Rights, * 1887, † 1976.

1969 INTERNATIONAL LABOUR ORGANIZATION – (ILO), Geneva.

1970 BORLAUG, NORMAN, U.S.A., International Maize and Wheat Improvement Center, Mexico City, * 1914.

1971 BRANDT, WILLY, Chancellor of the Federal Republic of Germany, * 1913.

1972 Reserved.

1973 The prize money for 1972 was allocated to the Main Fund.

The prize for 1973 was awarded jointly to:

KISSINGER, HENRY A., U.S.A., Secretary of State, State Department, Washington, * 1923, and

LE DUC THO, Democratic Republic of Viet Nam, * 1910. (Declined the prize).

1974 The prize was divided equally between:

MAC BRIDE, SEÁN, Ireland, President of the International Peace Bureau, Geneva, and the Commission of Namibia, United Nations, New York, * 1904, and

SATO, EISAKU, Japan, Prime Minister of Japan, * 1901, † 1975.

1975 SAKHAROV, ANDREI, USSR, * 1921.

1976 Reserved.

Mairead Corrigan

1977 The prize for 1976:

WILLIAMS, BETTY, Northern Ireland, Great Britain, * 1943; and

CORRIGAN, MAIREAD, Northern Ireland, Great Britain, * 1944.

The prize for 1977:

AMNESTY INTERNATIONAL, London.

1978 The prize for 1978 was divided equally between:

EL SADAT, MOHAMED ANWAR, Egypt, President of the Arab Republic of Egypt, * 1918 † 1981; and

BEGIN, MENACHEM, Israel, Prime Minister of Israel, * 1913 (in Brest Litovsk then Poland).

1979 MOTHER TERESA, Calcutta, India, * 1910 (Yugoslavia).

1980 PEREZ ESQUIVEL, ADOLFO, Argentine, * 1931.

1981 OFFICE OF THE UNITED NATIONS' HIGH COMMISSIONER FOR REFUGEES, Geneva, Switzerland.

1982 The prize was awarded jointly to:

MYRDAL, ALVA, Sweden, * 1902; and

GARCIA ROBLES, ALFONSO, Mexico, * 1911.

PRIZE-WINNERS IN ECONOMIC SCIENCES IN MEMORY OF ALFRED NOBEL

1969 The prize was awarded jointly to:

FRISCH, RAGNAR, Norway, Oslo University, * 1895, † 1973, and

TINBERGEN, JAN, The Netherlands, The Netherlands School of Economics, Rotterdam, * 1903: *"for having developed and applied dynamic models for the analysis of economic processes"*.

1970 SAMUELSON, PAUL, U.S.A., Massachusetts Institute of Technology, Cambridge, Mass., * 1915: *"for the scientific work through which he has developed static and dynamic economic theory and actively contributed to raising the level of analysis in economic science"*.

1971 KUZNETS, SIMON, U.S.A., Harvard University, Cambridge, Mass., * 1901 (in Russia): *"for his empirically founded interpretation of economic growth which has led to new and deepened insight into the economic and social structure and process of development"*.

1972 The prize was awarded jointly to:

HICKS, Sir JOHN R., Great Britain, All Souls College, Oxford, * 1904, and

ARROW, KENNETH J., U.S.A., Harvard University, Cambridge, Mass., * 1921: *"for their pioneering contributions to general economic equilibrium theory and welfare theory"*.

Kenneth Arrow

1973 LEONTIEF, WASSILY, U.S.A., Harvard University, Cambridge, Mass., * 1906 (in St Petersburg, Russia): *"for the development of the input-output method and for its application to important economic problems"*.

1974 The prize was divided equally between:

MYRDAL, GUNNAR, Sweden, * 1898, and

VON HAYEK, FRIEDRICH, AUGUST, Great Britain, * 1899 (in Vienna): *"for their pioneering work in the theory of money and economic fluctuations and for their penetrating analysis of the interdependence of economic, social and institutional phenomena"*.

1975 The prize was awarded jointly to:

KANTOROVICH, LEONID; U.S.S.R., Academy of Sciences, Moscow, * 1912, and

KOOPMANS, TJALLING C., U.S.A., Yale University, New Haven, Connecticut, * 1910 (in s' Graveland, the Netherlands): *"for their contributions to the theory of optimum allocation of resources".*

1976 FRIEDMAN, MILTON, U.S.A., University of Chicago, Chicago, Ill., * 1912: *"for his achievements in the fields of consumption analysis, monetary history and theory and for his demonstration of the complexity of stabilization policy".*

1977 The prize was divided equally between:

OHLIN, BERTIL, Sweden, Professor of Economics at the Stockholm School of Economics, Stockholm, * 1899, † 1979; and

MEADE, JAMES, Great Britain, Professor of Economics at Cambridge University, Cambridge, * 1907: *"for their pathbreaking contributions to the theory of international trade and inernational capital movements".*

1978 SIMON, HERBERT A., U.S.A., Carnegie-Mellon University, Pittsburgh, Pennsylvania, * 1916: *"for his pioneering research into the decision-making process within economic organizations".*

1979 The prize was divided equally between:

SCHULTZ, THEODORE W., U.S.A., University of Chicago, Ill., * 1902 and

LEWIS, Sir ARTHUR, United Kingdom, Princeton University, Princeton, U.S.A., * 1915 (West Indies): *"for their pioneering research into economic development research with particular consideration of the problems of development countries".*

1980 KLEIN, LAWRENCE R., U.S.A., University of Pennsylvania, Philadelphia, * 1920: *"for the creation of econometric models and their application to the analysis of economic fluctuations and economic policies".*

1981 TOBIN, JAMES, U.S.A., Yale University, New Haven, Connecticut, * 1918: *"for his analysis of financial markets and their relations to expenditure decisions, employment, production and prices".*

1982 STIGLER, GEORGE J., U.S.A., University of Chicago, Chicago, Illinois, * 1911: *"for his seminal studies of industrial structures, functioning of markets and causes and effects of public regulation".*

Assets

(Book Value) (Dec 31, 1980)	
Assets yielding interest	137,3 million Swedish kronor

Funds

(Dec 31, 1980)	
Main Fund (Prize Fund)	72,1 million Swedish kronor
Other Funds	34,6 million Swedish kronor
Total Funds	106,7 million Swedish kronor

Variations in the Funds

(in 1,000 Sw. kronor)	1901	1920	1940	1960	1970	1978	1980
Main Fund (Prize Fund)	27,716	30,191	33,337	37,598	44,293	51,189	72,068
Building Fund	1,180	2,227	781	560	890	1,364	1,201
Legacy Fund					–	618	585
Symposium Fund							3,569
Organization Funds:							
Physics	322	293	10	41	2,221	2,350	2,355
Chemistry	322	293	1,040	1,863	3,038	3,167	3,172
Medicine	324	140	2,068	–	92	139	173
Literature	217	209	446	451	522	594	606
Peace	324	99	496	210	551	329	181
Savings:							
Physics	29	528	1,091	991	2,739	2,580	2,773
Chemistry	29	544	1,138	929	1,590	1,397	1,580
Medicine	24	783	1,933	1,372	1,487	–	98
Literature	3	26	125	128	321	371	460
Peace	34	130	264	137	237	103	195
Economics						143	169

Special Funds:	1901	1920	1940	1960	1970	1978
Physics	–	140	482	901	1,323	2,931
Chemistry	–	419	1,024	1,515	1,917	3,465
Medicine	–	581	1,129	1,592	2,087	3,350
Literature	–	298	407	929	1,400	2,510
Peace	–	634	1,298	2,378	3,395	4,464

The Foundation was exempted from state income (with a few exceptions) in 1946. Until then about 13.5 million Swedish kronor had been paid in taxes. The Foundation, however, is not exempted from other taxes, local taxes and indirect taxes.

The following photographs have been furnished by;

The Nobel Foundation (pp 24, 28, 34, 44–45, 63)
Lars Tunbjörk/Bengt R Jansson (pp 40, 46, 47, 49)
Pressens Bild (pp 61, 86–110)
Reportagebild; Tobbe Gustavsson (p 62); Björn Elgstrand (p 65); (p 67)
Svenskt Pressfoto; Leif R Jansson (p 35); Stefan Lindblom (p 66)
Tiofoto; Nils-Johan Norelind (pp 48, 60); Lennart Olsson (p 64)